VEGAN SERENDIB

RECIPES FROM SRI LANKA

Copyright © 2022 by Mary Anne Mohanraj

Serendib Press
ISBN-13: 978-1-7330409-4-5

Illustrations by Pamudu Tennakoon
Book design by Jeremy John Parker

Photo Credits: Front cover by Mary Anne Mohanraj.

WWW.MARYANNEMOHANRAJ.COM
WWW.SERENDIBKITCHEN.COM

For Karina

VEGAN SERENDIB

RECIPES FROM SRI LANKA

Mary Anne Mohanraj

Illustrations by Pamudu Tennakoon

SERENDIB PRESS

CONTENTS

Introduction 1
Introduction from A Feast of Serendib 3

Ethnic Heritage and Colonial Influences 7
Sri Lankan Meals 7
A Few Caveats 9
Homesick 11

Spices and Ingredients 12
Master Recipe: Sri Lankan Curry Powder 18
Master Recipe: Seasoned Onions 20
Menu Suggestions 22
Kith and Kin 25

SAVORY ENTREES

Basic Approaches to Vegetables, Fruit, and Flowers 29

CURRY (cooked in coconut milk)
   Beet Curry 31
   Bottle Gourd and Spinach Curry 32
   Carrot Curry 34
   Cashew Curry / Kaju Kari 35
   Drumstick Curry / Murungakkai Kari 36
   Eggplant Curry / Kaththarikkai Kari 38

    Eggplant, Plantain, and Potato Curry / Kaliya Kari............40
    Fried Garlic Curry / Poritha Ulli Kari........................42
    Green Chili Curry / Kari Milaggai Kari......................44
    Green Mango Curry / Maankai Kari.........................46
    Green Jackfruit Curry / Palakkai Kari........................48
    Green Tomato and Lentil Curry.............................50
    Hibiscus (Shoeflower) Curry / Sembaruthipoo Kari............52
    Mild Green Plantain Curry.................................55
    Okra Curry / Vendikkai Kari................................57
    Pineapple Curry with Coconut Milk and Saffron..............59
    Pumpkin Curry...61
    Ripe Jackfruit Curry / Palapazham Kari......................63
    Spicy Plantain Curry......................................65

DEVILED (fried with cayenne, tomato, and onions)
    Deviled Potatoes / Urulai Kizhangu.........................67

PORIYAL (fried with seasoned onions)
    Asparagus Poriyal...69
    Brussels Sprouts Poriyal 71
    Cauliflower Poriyal 73
    Dried Hibiscus Poriyal 74
    Eggplant, Potato, and Pea Pod Poriyal 75
    Jaffna Whole Eggplant Fry / Yaalpana Kaththarikaii Poriyal 77
    Mixed Vegetable Poriyal...................................79

TEMPERED (cooked, mixed with seasoned onions)
    Tempered Lentils / Paruppu 81
    Tempered Potatoes..83

VARAI (steamed or stir-fried with coconut)
    Broccoli Varai 85
    Cabbage Varai / Muttaikoss Varai...........................87
    Green Bean Varai...88

SPECIAL PREPARATIONS
  Lime-Masala Mushrooms 89
  Marinated Ginger-Garlic Tofu
    (with Seitan and Tempeh Variations) 90
  Roasted Brussels Sprouts with Jaggery, Balsamic, & Cayenne 94
  Vegetable and Lentil Stew / Sambar 96

ACCOMPANIMENTS, SALADS, *and* SNACKS

FRIED SNACKS
  Bonda 104
  Chili-Mango Cashews / Kari-Maankai Kaju 106
  Lentil Patties / Kadalai Vadai 107
  Stir-fried Chickpea Snack / Kadalai Sundal 109
  Vegetable Cutlets 111

SALADS
  Cucumber Salad 113
  Pickled Beet Salad 114
  Rose (or Hibiscus) Salad / Rosappu Pachadi 115

CHUTNEYS
  Cranberry Rhubarb Chutney 117
  Green Coconut Chutney / Thengai Chutney 119
  Green Tomato Chutney with Apples 120
  Mango-Ginger Chutney 122

SAMBOLS
  Bitter Gourd Sambol / Paavakkai Sambol 124
  Chili Onion Sambol / Lunu Miris Sambol 125
  Coconut Sambol / Thengai-Poo, or Pol Sambol 126
  Eggplant Sambol / Kaththarikkai Sambol 128
  Ginger Sambol / Injii Sambol 129

Kale Sambol 130
Plantain Sambol 131
Rose Sambol 133
Sweet Onion Sambol / Seeni Sambol 134

Pickles
Eggplant Pickle / Brinjal Moju 136
Lime Pickle 138
Mango Pickle / Maankai Oorukkai 141
Quick-Pickled Cucumber-Carrot Relish 143
Spicy Pineapple Pickle / Achar 145

Special Dishes
Cucumber-Tomato Raita 146
Leeks Fried with Chili 147
Spiced Tomato Jam / Thakkaali Yaam 149

SOUPS

Coconut Milk Gravy / Sothi 152
Coriander Soup / Kothamalli Rasam 154
Curried Pumpkin Soup 156
Herbal Porridge / Kola Kenda 158

GRAINS

Biryani 162
Golden Rice Pilaf 164
Hoppers / Appam 165
Jaggery Pongal / Sakkarai Pongal 167
Kundu Thosai / Paniyaram 169
Milk Rice / Kiri Bath (with Bottle Gourd Variation) 172

Millet Roti, with Coconut and Jaggery / Kurakkan Roti 174
Red Rice Congee 176
Roti, Plain / Kothambu Roti 178
Roti Stir-Fry, Chopped / Kottu Roti. 179
Savory Rice Pancakes / Thosai 181
Spinach Pittu / Keerai Pittu 184
Steamed Rice Cakes / Idli 186
Steamed Rice Flour and Coconut / Arisi-Maa Pittu. 188
Steamed Rice Flour and Coconut with Milk / Pal Pittu 190
Stir-Fried Semolina / Uppuma 192
Stringhoppers / Idiyappam 194
Stringhopper Biryani / Idiyappam Biryani 197
Tamarind Rice with Black Lentils. 199

BEVERAGES

Beet Juice with Coconut Milk and Lime 202
Chai. 203
Cocktails 205
Falooda. 208
Mango Lassi 210
Mango-Passionfruit Punch or Mimosa 211
Fresh Sweet Lime Juice / Thesikkai Saaru 212
Spiced Yogurt Drink / Moru Thanni 213

SWEETS

Coconut Rock / Coconut Ice 216
Kokis. 218
Love Cake 220
Purple Yam Pudding or Porridge / Irasavalli Kizhangu Kanji ...222
Rich Cake (Wedding / Christmas Cake). 224

Sesame Balls / Ellu Urundai / Thala Guli 227
Sweet Coconut Steamed Appams / Halapa....................228
Sweet Thosai / Inippu Thosai 230
Tropical Fruit Salad with Ginger-Lime Dressing...............232
Tropical Fruit with Chili, Salt, and Lime 233

After-Dinner Digestive..234

Acknowledgements..235

Index..240

INTRODUCTION

I must begin this with a confession; I am not actually vegan. I'm not even vegetarian. Which begs the question—why would I write a vegan cookbook?

Really, it's because of Karina. A long time ago, I dated a girl who was vegetarian, leaning pretty close to vegan. We dated for three years, and in that time, we ate together a lot. She was vegetarian for ethical reasons, and so to avoid causing her distress, I ate vegetarian during that time as well. And it was just fine, at least while I was cooking for us at home, because I was mostly cooking Sri Lankan food, and there are lots of delicious vegetarian/vegan options in our cuisine. In Sri Lanka, we use coconut milk instead of dairy as a default, delectable vegetables and fruits are available year-round, and many Sri Lankans are vegetarian as part of their religious practice—for these reasons and more, the island has developed two thousand years of rich vegetarian/vegan culinary tradition.

It was a little harder to eat well—sometimes a lot harder—when we went out to restaurants together, or to parties at friends' homes. Often, the only vegetarian option was a salad, and a pretty boring salad at that—some leafy greens, probably a little wilted from sitting around, and a few shreds of carrot and slices of tomato. We'd go home still hungry, and sad about not getting to enjoy deliciousness.

It gave Karina so much pleasure when we found a restaurant that had tasty vegetarian options, especially foods she hadn't tried before. She's an adventurous eater, and when I took her to visit Sri Lanka for the first time, she researched and had a whole list of restaurants and foods she wanted to try. We were able to eat very well on our trip!

Flash forward to now—twenty years later, restaurants are slowly improving their vegetarian dishes, with more substantial offerings and a greater variety of them. But Sri Lankan cuisine is still hard to find in the U.S.—there are a few restaurants here and there, especially in New York, and if you go up to Toronto, you'll find plenty. But where I live, in Chicago, you pretty much have to drive eight hours up to St. Paul to find a Sri Lankan restaurant.

So this book is for everyone who wants to explore Sri Lankan vegan cuisine, whether you're vegan or not. Maybe you're doing Meatless Mondays, or you're exploring a more plant-based diet generally. Maybe you're looking for more sustainable ways to eat and exist on this planet, or maybe you're aiming towards a healthier diet. Maybe, like Karina, veganism is an ethical choice for you. Whatever the reason, what you'll find in these pages is an exciting and wildly varied cuisine, with a multitude of different preparations for vegetables, fruits, even flowers. You'll learn how to make a master recipe for roasted curry powder, and how to prepare seasoned onions to infuse your dishes with added flavor. You'll be invited to try a host of traditional preparations, which make up the bulk of the book, and also a few newer dishes, using ingredients that wouldn't have been available on the island in the old days—I experimented a bit with ingredients like vegan butter, vegan yogurt, and agar-agar in a few recipes.

Hopefully, this book will help make cooking and eating vegan cuisine easy, adventurous, fun, and most of all, fabulously delicious!

—*Mary Anne*

INTRODUCTION *from* A FEAST *of* SERENDIB

The first time I started writing a Sri Lankan cookbook, *A Taste of Serendib*, it was meant to simply be a Christmas present for my mother—writing down some of her recipes. The book offered a few recipes in each section, and featured sketches that a friend drew, illustrating me and my mother cooking, including a few choice quotes of my mother scolding me in the kitchen: "You cannot read and stir at the same time!"

It quickly spiraled into a book, but the focus was still simple—what little I knew of her recipes. It was designed to be accessible to college students, like the one I was at the time. I was an immigrant who had come to America very young, had grown up eating rice and curry every night, but had only a tenuous connection to the food culture of the homeland.

My mother had had to make many adaptations when she came to America in 1973. She used ketchup instead of tomatoes, for example, because she didn't have access to coconut milk, and other milks didn't have sufficient sweetness. (Ketchup also sped along the sauce-making process, since it's basically a cooked down mixture of tomatoes, vinegar, sugar, and salt.) My mother's recipes had already changed in America, and as I made them myself, they changed further, adapting to my tastes. When I gave my mother the finished book, she was pleased, but also immediately started pointing out where I'd gotten things wrong. I threatened to do a second edition of the book, with "Amma's corrections" all through it in red. I still think that would have been a good book, but she didn't go for it.

So the book stayed as it was for many years. It could have been left there. But instead, more than a decade later, I started working on a new cookbook, *A Feast of Serendib*.

My husband, Kevin, and I were talking recently about how I choose which projects to work on. There's often a pressure to spend my time and energy on more commercial projects, the ones that have the best odds of a good payout. This new cookbook should sell some copies; hopefully, it'll sell lots of copies. But it was hardly the most commercial project I could work on, and making the recipes, some of them over and over again, trying to get them right, was exceedingly time-consuming. If it were just about the money, that cookbook would make no sense at all.

But it's rarely just about the money. Over the years since I did the first cookbook, I've added more and more Sri Lankan recipes to my repertoire. My cookbook shelf has been overtaken by Sri Lankan cookbooks: from classics like the *Ceylon Daily News Cookbook*, to conflict-related books like the beautiful and heartbreaking *Handmade*, to fancy coffee table books full of glorious photos like *The Food of Sri Lanka*, to what is still my favorite, Charmaine Solomon's *Complete Asian Cookbook*—her Sri Lankan recipes taste like my mother's, like home.

I enjoy cooking dishes from other cuisines. Ethiopian is one of my favorites, and there are days when I crave sushi. Pizza is a family standby, and my children are built in large part out of pasta and broccoli. But I come back to Sri Lankan food—I cook it at least once or twice, most weeks. These days, I go online and read a dozen different recipes for a dish before I even start making it. I interrogate my Sri Lankan friends (both diasporan and homelander) about their recipes. I want to know how these dishes were typically made, in the villages, for generations and generations back. What should the balance of upu-puli (salty-sour) be? How thick do we want the finished gravy?

If I can't get a certain leafy green considered key to traditional cookery, I feel such frustration. But I try to accept the truth, that I will likely never cook exactly how homeland Sri Lankans would. My adaptations of my mother's adaptations are still tasty.

My husband is white American, for enough generations that he's not sure exactly where all his ancestors came from. Once, when Kevin and I were talking about naming our first child, about whether to give her a Tamil name, he asked whether we wouldn't be better off if we didn't cling so hard to ethnic, racial, nationalist traditions. Divisions. In some ways, I think he's right. Sri Lanka was riven by ethnic conflict for decades, and the country and its people are still dealing with the aftermath—it would be worth giving up much, if you could thereby make the conflicts end.

But this is who we are; this is what it is to be human. We are composed of our mother's hand with a salt shaker, the squeeze of fresh lime at the end of the dish. For those of us who are attenuated from the food of our grandparents and great-grandparents, learning how to cook this food, in its many iterations, can feel like filling a hole in your heart. We named our daughter Kaviarasi in the end, a very old Tamil name, which means 'queen of poetry.' Diasporic friends of my parents sent us thank you notes, for giving her such a classic Tamil name, for keeping the traditions alive.

I choose this. I choose to put time and energy into learning this food, into serving it to my mixed-race children, with the hopes that they will grow to love it too. Kavi comes into the kitchen to ask excitedly, "Oh, are you making curry?" When she asks for it, my heart skips a beat.

We come together with other Sri Lankans—homelander and diaspora, Sinhalese and Tamil, Buddhist and Hindu and Christian and Muslim—over delicious shared meals. Sri Lanka has been a multi-ethnic society for over two thousand years, with neighbors of different ethnicities, languages, religions, living side by side. We try to teach our children to be welcoming to all, to share our unique cultural traditions. That is part of what it means to be Sri Lankan, what it has always meant.

Can we choose the good parts of our culture to cherish, and leave the darker aspects behind? I hope so. I hope food can help provide a pathway there. Come together at our table, sharing milk rice and pol sambol, paruppu and jackfruit curry. Linger over the chai—just one more cup. Eat, drink, and share joy.

As for me, I make no claim to authenticity—there are many more authentic Sri Lankan cookbooks, painstakingly researched. But if there was a thin line drawn with that first cookbook, connecting me to the food of my ancestors, then the last few years of researching and adding recipe after recipe to this cookbook have thickened and strengthened the thread of connection, into a sturdy rope. One that you might use when lost, to find your way home.

I've come to appreciate the long history, the gathered wisdom of a thousand thousand cooks, who have known that with the perfection of hoppers at breakfast, all you need is a little fresh coconut sambol to accompany it. The more I cook these recipes, the more I grow to love this food.

I hope other readers of this cookbook will feel the same, and will love Sri Lanka, its food, and most of all, its people, along with me.

—Mary Anne Amirthi Mohanraj
August 2019

ETHNIC HERITAGE *and* COLONIAL INFLUENCES

My family is of the Tamil ethnic / cultural / language group, and almost all of the recipes that follow are Sri Lankan Tamil. (I have given Tamil names for some dishes, although for many, using English naming is common—my parents and their siblings will refer to cutlets, for example.) About sixteen percent of the Sri Lankan population is Tamil, a large percentage of whom came to Sri Lanka over two thousand years ago, settling primarily in the North and East; our cooking has diverged significantly from that of Indian Tamils from the southernmost state of Tamil Nadu.

Another group, the Hill Country / Indian Tamils, were brought over in the 19th and 20th centuries to work the coffee and tea plantations by the colonizers; some also came on their own as merchants and traders. The majority of the island's population is Sinhalese (about seventy-four percent), with a significant population of Moors (speaking Arabic-influenced Tamil, though many are also fluent in Sinhalese). There are also some smaller groups, including Malays and the indigenous Veddahs.

Sri Lanka experienced three waves of colonization—Portuguese (arriving 1505), Dutch (arriving 1602), and British (arriving 1802). All of the colonizing groups, along with the Hakka and Cantonese laborers they brought to Sri Lanka and more recent Chinese migrants, have left their culinary imprint on the island.

SRI LANKAN MEALS

I'm often asked what is characteristic of Sri Lankan food, and how it differs from Indian food. The second question is difficult, because it's usually Americans asking me, and they're used to Americanized Indian food, which is often fairly generic and watered down—not actual food from India, which is dramatically different, depending on whether you're talking Mughal-influenced North Indian cuisine, mostly-vegetarian Gujarati, etc.

Two main elements of Sri Lankan cuisine are our use of dark-roasted curry powder across the island and goraka (a souring fruit, similar to tamarind) in Sinhalese cooking. You won't find goraka in recipes here, though, as my Tamil family doesn't use it. Other characteristic elements include wholesome red rice, plenty of chili heat, curry leaves, lots of coconut milk and shredded coconut, and usually a touch of tang (from tomato, vinegar, tamarind, or lime). We do also eat a wide variety of non-vegetarian dishes, which I think is somewhat unusual in South Asia, given religious prohibitions, but can be traced to a long-standing multiethnic and multi-religious population. An island at the nexus of trade routes absorbs many culinary influences.

Sri Lankan cuisine has particularly strong similarities to Goan cuisine, in the Portuguese influence—more vinegar in the curries, plenty of coconut milk and coconut. Sri Lankan cuisine also has commonalities with South Indian cuisine—the dry spiced poriyals, the commonality of sambar and rasam (with plenty of tamarind), with idli, thosai, and uppuma for grain-based dishes.

I came to America when I was two years old, and so I never ate like a Sri Lankan would back home; for example, I had usually cereal for breakfast growing up in Connecticut. A typical Sri Lankan breakfast is some idli and sambar, or string hoppers and sothi, perhaps with paruppu (lentils). I grew up disliking lentils and have only recently learned to love them, but most people in Sri Lanka eat lots of lentils regularly. If you were feeling fancier, you might make hoppers for breakfast (but you'd have to plan that the night before). Uppuma is also a nice change, usually with some curry. I've gotten addicted to eating American pancakes with curry—the sweetness of the pancakes works really well with a spicy curry.

As a child, I would have often eaten a sandwich for lunch, but in Sri Lanka, lunches are rice and curries, often eaten around 3 p.m., and dinners are the same, often eaten around 9 p.m. Generally we would serve plain white rice, a curry or two, and a sambol or pickle. Appetizers and fancier accompaniments are usually saved for when guests or more family come over, although you'd likely keep containers of sambol or pickle around, for added flavor. Some of my American friends are surprised when I tell them that I had rice and curry for dinner every single night when I was growing up—what can I say? If your mother is an excellent cook, then you never get bored by a little repetition.

The fancier dishes, the hoppers and pittu and stringhoppers—those were all saved for parties. Usually, we stuffed ourselves on the delectable appetizers (called short eats), but somehow always managed to find room for dinner and then dessert. If you need one more little bite to fill out a table, some fresh fruit sprinkled with cayenne, salt, and lime is always appropriate as appetizer or accompaniment.

Note: Sri Lankans eat with their right hand, not with utensils, generally. It takes a little practice to learn how to make a neat little ball of rice and curry with your fingers, but more than a few of my friends have learned how over the years. Note that many of our recipes use whole spices such as cardamom pods, cloves, and cinnamon, that are not meant to be bitten into—when you're eating with your hands, it's easy to pick out and avoid those as you have dinner.

If you're planning on eating with a fork, you may want to either grind those spices before adding them, use pre-ground versions (generally not as strongly-flavored, so you may want a bit more), or tie them into a bit of loose-weave muslin that you can dig out before serving (this works better for a more liquid curry). If hosting a dinner party where guests will be eating with their hands, set a finger bowl at each place, so they can rinse and dry their fingers without leaving the table.

A FEW CAVEATS

I learned to cook from watching my mother; I would ask her how to make a dish, and she would say, "Just watch." So I did, and I wrote things down, and sometimes I would pester her with questions: when she tossed in some black mustard seed, I'd ask her how much she'd put in, and when she answered "three pinches," I'd estimate what that meant in teaspoons. I've tried to convert to standard measurements when I can, for your convenience (and if you need metric, I recommend using an online metric converter—if you tell it three cups, it'll tell you how many grams).

But I wouldn't recommend being too tied to the precise measurements in the recipes. Learning from my mother, I quickly found that it wasn't much use, trying to write down exact recipes. When I started cooking myself, I found that the appropriate amounts often varied from day to day, depending on a strange chemistry of interactions that I am not skilled enough to describe. Don't be afraid to add a little less cayenne, or a little more coconut milk or ketchup, or vice versa!

Homesick

The problem with going deep
is that you can fall in.

You find yourself reheating
frozen food, a pale imitation
of the real thing. Making
other dishes over and over
trying to remember
decades-old cinnamon
in the nose, lime on the tongue,
chili heat lingering on your lips—
a pain that you seek out repeatedly.

Sometimes you think your heart
can't take it; it would be easier
to order pasta instead.

Yet here you are, microwaving
frozen hoppers that you keep
stashed in the basement
deep freeze. Hoarded for
those days when you need
them, even if it hurts.

SPICES *and* INGREDIENTS

AGAR-AGAR is a powder. You can often find it at a large organic gourmet store, like Whole Foods, or possibly at your local Indian grocery store.

If you can't find BLACK (OR BROWN) MUSTARD SEED, regular mustard seed will do.

CARDAMOM PODS are available green, white, or black—you want the green cardamom pods (the ones commonly found in American grocery stores) for Sri Lankan cuisine. We generally use them whole in curries, though do be careful not to bite into them when you eat, as they can be unpleasant; if you're worried, you can always tie whole spices into a bit of cheesecloth and let that simmer in a curry sauce, removing before serving. You can also toast the pods, let them cool, and then crack them open and just use the seeds, though that's quite labor intensive. Ground cardamom powder is less flavorful; it loses flavor quickly on grinding.

Buy your CAYENNE at the Indian grocery store if you can—it should be a dark red, and is usually much hotter than American grocery store cayenne. (It may even be labeled in varieties, such as Hot or Extra Hot). If you can't get to such a store, or order it online, use crushed dried red chili pods—Mexican chili (a mix of several spices) is not a good substitute. Generally, you'll want to fry the cayenne for a few seconds in a little hot oil, before adding curry powder or other spices, or it will taste raw in the finished dish. If you start to cough, that's a warning that the cayenne is about to burn. Some recipes will also call for DRIED RED CHILIES, with similar flavor and heat, but different consistency.

TRUE CEYLON CINNAMON is grown in Sri Lanka, and is generally considered higher quality than the cassia cinnamon (hard, tight sticks, difficult to grind) that is much more commonly available. But you can certainly use either in these dishes.

An essential spice for Sri Lankan cooking are CLOVES—use these aromatic flower buds whole in most curries, or powdered in desserts.

CORIANDER SEED is one of the oldest known spices in the world, very aromatic with citrus notes. Dry roast it to release additional flavor, until it turns golden-brown and starts 'popping' in the pan.

Many of my dishes start with sautéing CUMIN SEEDS in oil with onions; cumin has a strong fragrance and lends an essential smoky note to the dishes. If you toast it, be careful to stir on low heat—cumin burns very easily, and would then be quite bitter in your dish.

CURRY LEAVES are broad, level, dark-green leaves, thumb-sized or larger, which can be found in a good Indian grocery store, either fresh, frozen, or dried, and which are becoming more available in regular American grocery stores. There is no good substitute—if you can't find them, leave them out of the recipe. The thin, rounded silvery leaves of the *curry plant* you can occasionally find at garden stores are not meant for cooking—they merely smell curry-like. You can now buy curry leaves online, through Amazon and elsewhere. If they arrive fresh and it's more than you can use, freeze the extra (you can just add them frozen to a curry, without thawing first). If they arrive dried, they won't be quite as strong, so use a bit more. My recipes generally call for a dozen curry leaves; this is an estimate, and a few more or less won't matter.

Sri Lankan cooking is often hotter than Indian; if you're not used to it, trying making the recipe with only half the roasted CURRY POWDER and/or cayenne the first time around. Indian curry powder is not a good substitute for Sri Lankan; look for Sri Lankan or Jaffna roasted curry powder online or in stores for these recipes, or make your own, following the recipe provided. This is *key* to getting the flavors right.

Never buy your SHREDDED COCONUT in the baking aisle—it's almost certainly sweetened. Try the Indian grocery or the bulk foods section of your local grocery store instead. If you can find frozen shredded coconut, even better; it will have a fresher taste. Or, if you want, you can buy whole coconut and a coconut grater to (laboriously) grate your own, as my mother did.

Another essential spice is FENNEL SEED, offering a sweet, grassy flavor with notes of anise and licorice. It's supposedly good for your digestion, and candy-coated fennel seeds are also used as a mouth freshener after meals.

FENUGREEK is the same as methi seed, which you can generally find in an Indian grocery store (where, incidentally, most spices will be much cheaper than in your general grocery store).

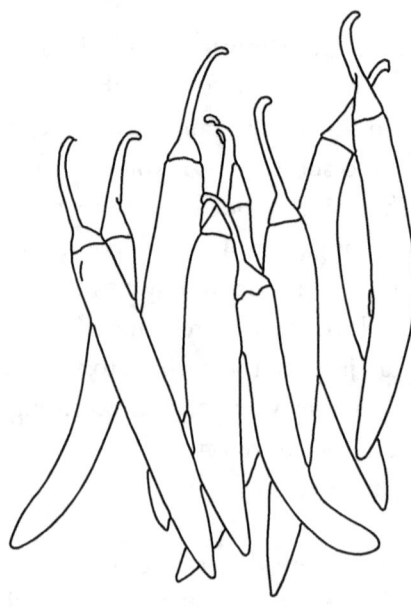

When a recipe calls for GREEN CHILIES, it's asking for finger hot chilies, which are slender and about a finger-length, with a delicious flavor. (They do ripen to red if left on the plant, and can still be used in these dishes.) These chilies are quite hot, so if you can't find them and substitute in something like jalapeño, you'll want to use more chili. Serrano chilies are a decent substitute; you can also use Thai green chilies for similar heat, but they offer less of the green chili flavor. I store green chilies in the freezer in a big Ziploc bag, and just chop a few of them, still frozen, as needed for Sri Lankan dishes. (Carefully remove the seeds if you're looking for less heat. Wash your hands afterwards!)

IDLI RICE is a specific kind of Indian rice that is parboiled. Parboiled (or converted) rice is rice that has been partially boiled in the husk, through a process of soaking, steaming, and drying. These steps make rice easier to process by hand, boost its nutritional profile (parboiling drives nutrients, especially thiamin, from the bran to the endosperm), and change its texture. (They also reduce its cooking time and make it resistant to weevils.)

JAGGERY is a traditional sugar made from the concentrated sap of palm trees. It comes in a range of shades of brown, and it is delicious. If jaggery is not available, brown sugar + a little molasses will approximate the flavor.

One of the questions I get asked most often is, "Really, KETCHUP?" Yes, really. My mother used it, and so can you. If you'd really rather not, though, you can use chopped tomatoes, vinegar, salt, and sugar, cooked down to a sauce. (Which is basically ketchup.)

If you're looking for a fine, fresh, lemony tang with hints of ginger and mint, LEMONGRASS is the herb for you. Buy stalks that are fragrant, tightly formed, and a lemony-green color. If they're loose, brown, or crumbling, they're old and won't lend much flavor to your dish. I often grow lemongrass with my other herbs—since it's a tropical, it does need to come inside for the winter in Chicago! It can also often be found frozen in the grocery store.

You must also have LIME JUICE on hand (lemon may be substituted if lime isn't available), as balancing sweet-salt-tang-spice is key to Sri Lankan cuisine. Too many times when I was first learning to cook, I made a dish, served it to guests, was frustrated that it wasn't quite as tasty as it should be—and realized I'd forgotten to add the lime!

Many of the recipes call for a little MILK—you can use any vegan milk you like; coconut milk is a little sweeter and much richer in taste than most due to the high fat content. You can sometimes find light coconut milk, which is not terrible. I've used rice milk, almond milk, and soy milk, and while the dish won't thicken as much as with coconut milk, it still basically works.

I keep a little jar of ground black pepper on hand for dishes that need a teaspoon or more—I buy strongly-flavored Tellicherry PEPPERCORNS from Penzeys online (www.penzeys.com), grind them in a coffee grinder I keep dedicated for spices (although you can use a regular coffee grinder if you clean it out thoroughly), and grind up a jar's worth as needed. The flavor is much better than you'd get from the pre-ground black pepper at the grocery store.

My friend Roshani cooks many of her dishes using RAMPÉ, which is also known as pandan leaf; I never got in the habit of cooking with it, as it was quite hard to find when I was learning to cook. But it's commonly used in Sri Lankan cooking, and a simple way to add it is to drop a leaf into a pot of rice while cooking, where it will lend a lovely aroma; you can also add a few pieces to a curry.

If you don't have ROSE ESSENCE, you can substitute rose water, which is more readily available in stores. It contains a lot more water, obviously, so adjust other ingredients for pleasing result. Just be careful—the essence is extremely strong. A rough conversion is 5ml rose essence = 15ml rose water, or 1 tsp. rose essence = 1 Tbsp. rose water. You can also buy rose essence online.

There are many recipes for South Indian SAMBAR POWDER available online, but I admit, this one I buy pre-mixed. It's typically a blend of chili, coriander, curry leaves, fenugreek, chana dal, cumin, peppercorn, asafetida, and similar spices.

TAMARIND, a tangy fruit, comes in many forms—blocks of hard paste, fresh pods, dried pods—and the form I prefer, a soft concentrated paste which comes in a small jar (generally with a red lid). Again, the Indian grocery store is your friend.

When soaked in water, the seeds of several basil varieties (TULSI SEEDS) become gelatinous, and are used in Sri Lankan (and other Asian) drinks and desserts, such as falooda.

URAD DAL is also known as black gram / matpe bean / ulunththu. The product sold as BLACK LENTIL is usually the whole urad bean, whereas the split bean (the interior being white) is called WHITE LENTIL. It should not be confused with the much smaller true black lentil (*Lens culinaris*). Generally in these recipes, I'll be using split urad dal, which has been washed and the husks removed; it appears primarily white in color.

VINEGAR is another way to add that characteristic tang to Sri Lankan dishes. White vinegar is standard, though these days, rice wine vinegar is also widely used, with its subtle, delicately sweet flavor. Some Sri Lankan cooks today will even use sushi vinegar, to get that additional sweet note to a dish without the extra step of adding sugar.

MASTER RECIPE: Sri Lankan Curry Powder

One of the main characteristics of Sri Lankan cooking is that the spices are dark roasted. You cannot simply substitute yellow curry powder! If your local Indian grocery store carries Jaffna Curry Powder, that's from northern Sri Lanka and an excellent option; it can also be found online. Or you can always make your own.

- 1 cup coriander seeds
- ½ cup cumin seeds
- 1 Tbsp. fennel seeds
- 1 rounded tsp. fenugreek seeds (a.k.a. methi seeds)
- 1 2-inch cinnamon stick
- 1 rounded tsp. whole cloves
- 1 rounded tsp. cardamom seeds
- 2 Tbsp. dried curry leaves
- 2 rounded tsp. cayenne

1. In a dry pan over medium heat, roast separately the coriander, cumin, fennel, and fenugreek, stirring constantly until each one becomes a fairly dark brown.

Note: Do not attempt to save time by roasting them together—they each have different cooking times and you will only end up half-cooking some and burning others.

2. Put into blender container (I use a coffee grinder that is dedicated solely to spice grinding) together with cinnamon stick broken in pieces, the cloves, cardamom, and curry leaves.

3. Blend at high speed until finely powdered. Sieve into a bowl, discarding any large pieces, and combine with cayenne; stir well. Store in airtight jar.

MASTER RECIPE:
Sri Lankan Seasoned Onions

Many of our dishes start with cooking onions in oil with ginger, garlic, black mustard seed, and cumin seed, so I wanted to take the time to go through that process in a little more detail. Do chop the onions finely; they'll be breaking down to make the base for your sauce, and if they're in big pieces, they'll take much longer to break down into a proper sauce.

A great time-saver, if you're making my curries often, is to do a double (or triple, or quadruple) batch of this, maybe on a lazy Sunday, and then divide and freeze the extra. It means that on a weekday night when you're in a hurry, you can grab a frozen bag of seasoned onions, toss them in a hot pan, and within minutes be adding your vegetables, cutting your weeknight cooking time in half.

Also, you can buy chopped ginger-garlic paste in the Indian stores, which is helpful for when you're in a hurry—I'd use about 2 tablespoons in this recipe. It's not quite as good as chopping fresh, but is an acceptable substitute for everyday cooking.

- 3 medium yellow onions, chopped fine
- 3 Tbsp. vegetable oil
- 1-2 Tbsp. ginger, chopped fine
- 1 tsp. black mustard seed
- 1 tsp. cumin seed
- 3-5 cloves garlic, chopped fine

Optional first step: Sauté black mustard seed in oil to make mustard oil—this will add an extra little hit of flavor, but I admit, I mostly don't bother with this unless I'm being extra fancy; I add the seeds together later on.

1. Sauté onions in oil until translucent. Now, you can cook them on high or medium-high, stirring constantly, if you have your other ingredients ready. But I tend to do this step on medium or even low, so I can stir only occasionally, in between chopping ginger, garlic, and any other ingredients.

2. Add black mustard seed, cumin seed, and ginger; sauté a few minutes more. (This is when I'd be chopping my garlic.) If you need more oil, feel free to add it at this point.

3. Add garlic and cook, stirring occasionally, a few more minutes, until golden-translucent. Garlic burns easily, so you don't want to add it early on, especially when you just have hot oil in the pan. Much safer to add it at this stage.

That's it! You'll almost always be adding fresh curry leaves next, with pieces of cinnamon stick, cardamom pods, and cloves, and then going on to cayenne, roasted curry powder, and salt, but this is a good point to pause, divide, and freeze anything you're not using right away. You can also add the other ingredients and freeze at that point, if you're planning to use them for particular curries that call for them. Be sure to squeeze as much air as possible out of the plastic bag, to avoid freezer burn.

MENU SUGGESTIONS

LIGHT *and* CLASSIC BREAKFAST:
- stringhoppers with coconut milk gravy and coconut sambol
- herbal porridge with fresh fruit

WEEKNIGHT SUPPER:
- green jackfruit or eggplant curry with kale sambol, pickled beet salad, and rice

TO DELIGHT CHILDREN:
- pineapple curry, tempered lentils, or green bean varai, with cauliflower poriyal and rice (for dinner)
- mango lassi or beet juice (to drink)
- many options for sweets: kokis, coconut rock, sweet thosai, tropical fruit salad

TO TAKE ON *a* PICNIC *or* ON *the* ROAD:
- chili-mango cashews, vegetable cutlets, lentil patties

UNUSUAL TECHNIQUES *to* TRY:
- Mains: hoppers, biryani, stringhoppers, chopped roti stir-fry, pittu, uppuma
- Various: bonda, stir-fried chickpea snack, Jaffna whole eggplant fry, tempered lentils

A SMALL DINNER PARTY:
- spiced tomato jam, cranberry rhubarb chutney, with vegan cheese and crackers

- eggplant, plantain, and potato curry, asparagus poriyal & kale sambol
- golden rice pilaf, biryani, stringhoppers or pittu
- mango lassi, beet juice or spiced yogurt drink, chai, cocktails
- purple yam pudding or tropical fruit salad (with vegan ice cream!)

BRUNCH *with* FRIENDS:

- hoppers or pittu
- sweet onion sambol, chili onion sambol, and green coconut chutney
- jackfruit or plantain (mild or spicy) curry
- tropical fruit salad with ginger-lime dressing
- mango-passionfruit mimosas

POTLUCK FAVORITES:

- cashew curry, eggplant, potato, and peapod poriyal, tempered lentils, kale sambol
- biryani or stringhopper biryani
- coconut rock or love cake

COCKTAIL PARTY:

- arrack sour, beetroot cocktail, Ceylon sunrise, mango-passionfruit punch
- chili-mango cashews, bonda, and/or stir-fried chickpea snack
- vegetable cutlets & lentil patties
- spiced tomato jam, cranberry rhubarb chutney, with vegan cheese and crackers
- coconut rock, love cake, purple yam pudding

VEGAN FEAST (*to feed twenty to thirty*):

- chili-mango cashews, vegetable cutlets, & lentil patties
- beet or cashew curry
- drumstick, okra, or eggplant, plantain, and potato curry
- green tomato and lentil curry or tempered lentils

- ripe jackfruit, pineapple, or mild/spicy plantain curry
- deviled or tempered potatoes
- broccoli, cabbage, or green bean varai
- eggplant or kale sambol
- pittu and/or rice
- beet juice, fresh sweet lime juice, and/or spiced yogurt drink
- coconut rock, love cake, purple yam pudding, and/or sesame balls

ROYAL FEAST (*to feed two hundred or so*):

Appetizers:
- bonda, chili-mango cashews, stir-fried chickpea snack, vegetable cutlets, lentil patties

Mains and Sides:
- beet curry & cashew curry
- drumstick or okra curry
- ripe jackfruit, pineapple, or mild/spicy plantain curry
- green tomato and lentil curry or tempered lentils
- deviled or tempered potatoes
- broccoli, cabbage, or green bean varai
- asparagus or cauliflower poriyal
- Jaffna whole eggplant fry
- leeks fried with chili or lime-masala mushrooms
- pol sambol, leeks fried with chili, mango pickle
- bitter gourd, eggplant, and/or kale sambol
- cucumber salad, pickled beet salad and/or rose salad
- eggplant, lime, and/or mango pickle
- biryani, milk rice, or tamarind rice, roti or coconut roti, pittu, and/or stringhopper biryani
- beet juice, fresh sweet lime juice, and/or spiced yogurt drink

Desserts:
- All of them!

Kith and Kin

hair, clothes, and kitchen
redolent with roasted spices
cooking deep into the night
with children and husband asleep
this much unchanged, untranslated

I stand over the pan, stirring
low and slow, singing to amuse
myself—haste would destroy
the spell of memory, consanguinity
coriander cumin fennel fenugreek
in order of decreasing amount
cinnamon cloves cardamom
curry leaves and chili powder

if I have to look up the ingredients
every time, am I insufficiently
authentic? eventually, I will grind
knowledge into my bones

Ammama, could you have guessed
your granddaughter would live
half a world away, would structure
love so differently, would pass your
recipes to a thousand strangers?

in the old days, recipes were hoarded
like gold bangles; a dowry locked
in your mind could not be stolen;
now I give them away, scatter them
like kisses on the networked seas

I suspect it would frighten you,
what a daughter might give away
might lose forever. yet perhaps
the world is changing. a woman
may give herself away, undiminished

trust me. what the seas carried
away, they will return; your children's
children are with you
though at times unrecognizable

bend down your head and breathe
deep, roasting scents tangled in my hair
see—you know me still. some things
come back to you, a thousandfold

SAVORY ENTREES

CURRY
(cooked in coconut milk)

Beet Curry
Bottle Gourd and Spinach Curry
Carrot Curry
Cashew Curry / Kaju Kari
Drumstick Curry / Murungakkai Kari
Eggplant Curry / Kaththarikkai Kari
Eggplant, Plantain, and Potato Curry / Kaliya Kari
Fried Garlic Curry / Poritha Ulli Kari
Green Chili Curry / Kari-Milaggai Kari
Green Mango Curry / Maankai Kari
Green Jackfruit Curry / Palakkai Kari
Green Tomato and Lentil Curry
Hibiscus (Shoeflower) Curry / Sembaruthipoo Kari
Mild Green Plantain Curry
Okra Curry / Vendikkai Kari
Pineapple Curry with Coconut Milk and Saffron
Pumpkin Curry
Ripe Jackfruit Curry / Palapazham Kari
Spicy Plantain Curry

DEVILED
(fried with cayenne, tomato, and onions)

Deviled Potatoes / Urulai Kizhangu

PORIYAL

(fried with seasoned onions)

Asparagus Poriyal
Brussels Sprouts Poriyal
Cauliflower Poriyal
Dried Hibiscus Poriyal
Eggplant, Potato, and Pea Pod Poriyal
Jaffna Whole Eggplant Fry / Yaalpana Kaththarikaii Poriyal
Mixed Vegetable Poriyal

TEMPERED

(cooked, mixed with seasoned onions)

Tempered Lentils / Paruppu
Tempered Potatoes

VARAI

(steamed or stir-fried with coconut)

Broccoli Varai
Cabbage Varai / Muttaikoss Varai
Green Bean Varai

SPECIAL PREPARATIONS

Lime-Masala Mushrooms
Marinated Ginger-Garlic Tofu (with Seitan and Tempeh Variations)
Roasted Brussels Sprouts with Jaggery, Balsamic, and Cayenne
Vegetable and Lentil Stew / Sambar

BASIC APPROACHES *to* VEGETABLES, FRUIT, *and* FLOWERS

CURRY *(cooked in coconut milk):* This is a standard curry approach—sauté onions with spices, add vegetables and coconut milk, simmer until cooked.

DEVILED *(fried with cayenne, tomato, and onions):* Deviled potatoes are delicious, and I would imagine that you could approach many other vegetables the same way.

PORIYAL *(sautéed with seasoned onions):* Poriyal is a Tamil dish consisting of sautéed and spiced shredded vegetables. Similar dishes appear in other parts of South Asia, under different names.

TEMPERED *(cooked, mixed with seasoned onions):* I used to be really confused when my mom referred to 'tempered potatoes' or other tempered dishes. In Western cooking, 'tempering' means to slowly bring up the temperature of a cold or room temperature ingredient, by adding small amounts of a hot or boiling liquid. Adding the hot liquid gradually prevents the cool ingredient from cooking or setting. In Western cooking, tempering typically refers to either chocolate or eggs.

In South Asian cuisine, tempering is a widely used cooking method; you heat spices in hot oil, and then add them to your dish at the end of cooking. The hot oil extracts the flavors of the spices and intensifies their effect. South Asian tempering is done either at the beginning of the cooking process or as a final flavoring at the end—or sometimes both! The ingredients are usually added in rapid succession, rarely together, with those requiring longer cooking added earlier and those requiring less cooking added later. For instance, you'd add black mustard seeds to the hot oil first and then later add chopped garlic, which could burn if added earlier.

You can use this method with a wide variety of spices, for a wide variety of vegetables; you can simply mix tempered onions with boiled potatoes, or add them to a simmered lentil curry. Tempering highlights flavors that have already cooked into the dish, adding a bright, fresh seasoning note.

VARAI *(steamed or stir-fried with coconut):* A varai is a mixture of greens and coconut traditionally cooked in a dry skillet. Some recipes use a little oil, but generally, this is a light, healthy way to cook vegetables. In Sri Lanka, a varai is often made with the leaves of plants not found in American grocery stores, but it can be prepared with broccoli, cauliflower, collard greens, mustard greens, cabbage, etc.

The greens are often cooked without any oil, so the only fat comes from the coconut. I strongly recommend using fresh or frozen rather than dried coconut if possible (and definitely not sweetened), because the flavor and taste will be much better. But if dried is all you have, rehydrate it in a little heated coconut milk beforehand.

Often, a greens dish will be made as a fresh sambol first, for lunch, and then what remains will be turned into a varai, which will keep better, and may be eaten with dinner, or at breakfast the next morning.

Beet Curry

(30 minutes, serves 4)

This dish has a lovely sweet flavor with just a hint of spice—beets have a higher sugar content than any other vegetable. The lime tang beautifully balances the sweetness and the spice, for a flavor characteristic of Sri Lankan cuisine.

> 3 medium onions, chopped fine
> 3 Tbsp. vegetable oil
> ¼ tsp. black mustard seed
> ¼ tsp. cumin seed
> 4 large beets (about 1 lb.), peeled, cut in thick matchsticks
> 1–2 rounded tsp. salt
> 1 rounded tsp. ground turmeric
> 2–3 tsp. lime juice
> 1–3 chopped green chilies
> 2 dozen curry leaves, optional
> 2 cups coconut milk

1. Sauté onions in oil on high with mustard seed and cumin seeds until onions are golden / translucent (not brown). Add beets, salt, turmeric, lime juice, chilies, and curry leaves. Continue cooking on high about 10–15 minutes, stirring occasionally, just enough so the onions and beets don't burn—you want that beautifully caramelized flavor coming through.

2. Lower heat to medium and add coconut milk. Cook, stirring frequently, until beets are cooked through and coconut milk has reduced to simply coating the beets, about 10 minutes. Serve hot.

Bottle Gourd (or Cucumber) and Spinach Curry

(25 minutes, serves 4)

Bottle gourds are one of the original immigrating foods, their seeds drifting across the ocean and making their way from Africa around the world to North America, South America, and Asia, over 10,000 years ago. Amazing!

Because bottle gourd (*Lagenaria siceraria*) is also called calabash, they're sometimes confused with the hard, hollow fruits of the unrelated calabash tree (*Crescentia cujete*).

Bottle gourd flesh is mild, very similar to cucumbers, but a little sweeter. Young seeds and bottle gourd skin are also edible, so you might want to save those for other dishes. But for this curry, you'll be working with the flesh of the vegetable.

This is a simple curry on its own (lots of spices, but very few steps!), and can be easily varied by adding eggplant, lentils, or in this case, fresh spinach. Bottle gourd also makes a nice stir-fry (varai), or soup.

> 2 Tbsp. vegetable oil
> 3–4 shallots (or red onion), finely chopped
> 2 cloves garlic, crushed
> 1 tsp. mustard seeds
> 1 tsp. cumin seeds
> 1 tsp. fenugreek seeds
> 1 stalk curry leaves (about a dozen)
> 1 green chilli pepper, thinly sliced
> ½ tsp. turmeric powder
> ½ tsp. cayenne (or to taste)

½ tsp. Sri Lankan roasted curry powder
1 tsp. salt
4 cups (about 300 grams) bottle gourd (or cucumber), peeled, seeds removed and discarded, and chopped or shredded
2 cups coconut milk
1–2 Tbsp. lime juice (about ½–1 lime)
1 bag baby spinach leaves (about 4 oz.), optional

1. Heat oil in a pot, and add onions, garlic, spices, and bottle gourd. Sauté, stirring occasionally, for 10–15 minutes, until onions are golden and a little browned.

2. Add coconut milk and simmer 5 minutes, stir in lime juice, then add spinach if using, and simmer 5–10 minutes more. Serve hot, with rice or bread.

Carrot Curry

(20 minutes, serves 4)

This carrot curry is a perfect dish for early spring, and is the perfect accompaniment for jackfruit or chickpea curry. For a variation, you can switch out half the carrots for green beans, which brings a pleasant contrast and some extra nutrition to your plate.

> 3 medium onions, chopped
> 3 Tbsp. vegetable oil
> ¼ tsp. black mustard seed
> ¼ tsp. cumin seed
> 6 large carrots, peeled and cut into coins
> 1 rounded tsp. salt
> 1 rounded tsp. ground turmeric
> ½–1 cup coconut milk

1. Sauté onions in oil on high with mustard seed and cumin seeds until onions are golden. Add carrots, turmeric, and salt. Cook on medium-high, stirring, until carrots are mostly cooked, about 10 minutes.

2. Add coconut milk and turn heat down to low; simmer until the sauce thickens, stirring frequently, about 3–5 more minutes. Be careful not to curdle the milk by cooking on high heat. Serve hot.

Cashew Curry / Kaju Kari

(1 hour, serves 4–6)

Cashews are relatively expensive, compared to most vegetables; this is a luscious dish served to vegetarian dinner guests, unctuous and rich.

> 3 medium onions, diced
> 3 Tbsp. vegetable oil
> ¼ tsp. black mustard seed
> ¼ tsp. cumin seed
> 8–12 curry leaves
> 1 2-inch cinnamon stick
> 1 Tbsp. Sri Lankan curry powder
> 1 lb. roasted, salted cashews
> 1 can coconut milk
> 1 Tbsp. lime juice
> salt to taste (about ½–1 tsp.)

3. In a large pot, sauté onions in oil on medium-high with mustard seed, cumin seed, curry leaves, and cinnamon stick, until onions are golden / translucent (not brown). Add curry powder, cashews, and coconut milk.

4. Lower heat to medium. Cover and cook, stirring periodically, until cashews are soft and sauce is thick, about 30 minutes. Remove cover, taste, and add salt if desired. Add lime juice; simmer a few additional minutes, stirring. Serve hot.

Note: Traditionally, you'd start with raw whole cashews and soak them for two hours before cooking, which makes for a more tender finished product. I'm perfectly happy with the results from roasted, salted cashews.

Drumstick Curry / Murungakkai Kari

(1 hour, serves 4–6)

Drumsticks (*Moringa oleifera*) are extremely popular vegetables in Sri Lanka and South Asia, and are reputed to have many health benefits. They're commonly prepared for women during and after pregnancy, and are said to help heal wounds and ease the discomfort of childbirth; midwives claim they help with post-partum depression as well. The preparation below is a tangy-spicy approach, though drumsticks are also commonly cooked in a mild yellow curry preparation.

Drumsticks are a vegetable that I've been unable so far to find fresh in Chicagoland, so I make this from frozen; you can also use canned. This would be tricky to eat with knife and fork, because you really need to scrape the flesh of the vegetable off the tough, fibrous exterior stalk with your teeth, so I recommend eating these with your hand, served with rice. Alternatively, you can chew them to get out all the flavor, and then discard the fibrous remains.

I recommend serving drumsticks with lentils, chickpeas, or something else fairly substantial, as there's not a lot of 'meat' for the bulk of the dish. Plenty of deliciousness, though!

> 1 lb. frozen drumsticks (or 4 long fresh drumsticks, cut to roughly 3-inch pieces)
> ¼ cup oil
> 2 medium onions, chopped
> 1 tsp. fenugreek seeds
> 1 stalk curry leaves
> 2 Tbsp. ginger, minced

6 cloves garlic, chopped
3 green chilies, sliced lengthwise
3 tsp. Sri Lankan curry powder
1 tsp. salt
2 cups water
1 cup coconut milk
½ tsp. tamarind paste

1. Heat oil in a large frying pan, and fry drumsticks for a few minutes, browning the exteriors; remove to a dish.

2. Add onions, fenugreek, curry leaves, ginger, garlic, and chilies to the oil, and sauté until onions are golden-brown.

3. Add drumsticks back to pan, with curry powder, salt, and water; cover and cook until drumsticks are tender, about twenty minutes.

4. Stir in coconut milk and tamarind, and simmer for a few more minutes, until well blended. Serve hot with rice.

Eggplant Curry / Kaththarikkai Kari

(30 minutes draining time + 30 minutes, serves 6)

My mother's eggplant curry was always a huge hit at Sri Lankan dinner parties, and is particularly popular with vegetarians.

1 lb. eggplant, roughly 1-inch cubes
1 tsp. ground turmeric
1 tsp. salt
2 onions, chopped coarsely
½ cup oil
1 tsp. cumin seed
1 tsp. black mustard seed
1 dozen curry leaves
1 tsp. brown sugar
1 tsp. Sri Lankan curry powder
½ cup coconut milk

1. Prep eggplant—rub with turmeric and salt and then set in a colander to drain at least 30 minutes, which will draw out the bitter water. Blot dry with paper towels.

2. Sauté onions in oil on medium-high, stirring, with cumin seed, black mustard seed, and curry leaves, until golden.

3. Add eggplant, sugar, and curry powder, and sauté for another ten minutes or so, until eggplant is nicely fried. (Add more oil if needed.)

4. Add coconut milk and simmer for a few minutes until well blended. Serve hot with rice or roti—particularly nice for a vegetarian dinner with lentils as the main protein.

Variation: Eggplant and bell pepper work well together in this dish; just add chopped bell pepper about five minutes into frying the eggplant for a nice sweet element to the dish. Sometimes I make a nightshade curry, adding potatoes and tomatoes as well—small cubed potatoes would go into the onions first, then eggplant and spices, then bell pepper, then tomato, with a few minutes between each addition.

Eggplant, Plantain, and Potato Curry / Kaliya Kari

(40 minutes, serves 4)

A traditional Sri Lankan curry from our Muslim community, featuring fried eggplant, plantain, and potato, simmered in a rich coconut milk curry.

- 1 large eggplant, cubed
- 2 plantains, cut into similar sized pieces
- 5–7 small potatoes, cubed
- 1 tsp. turmeric, 2 pinches of salt, dissolved into 2–3 cups water, divided into two bowls
- vegetable oil for deep frying
- 1 large onion, sliced thin
- ½ cup vegetable oil
- 1 Tbsp. ginger, minced
- 3 garlic cloves, minced
- 3 cloves
- 3 cardamom pods
- 1 cinnamon stick, broken into pieces
- 1 stalk curry leaves (about a dozen)
- 1 inch pandan leaf (optional)
- 1 Tbsp. Sri Lankan roasted curry powder
- 1 tsp. cayenne (optional)
- 1 Tbsp. jaggery or dark brown sugar
- 1 tsp. tamarind paste
- 1 tsp. salt
- ½ cup + 1 ½ cups coconut milk
- 2–3 cups water (enough to cover)

1. To prevent discoloration and add a little flavor, once you cube eggplant and plantains, submerge them (separately) in bowls of water, each seasoned with ½ tsp. turmeric and pinch of salt.

2. Heat oil for deep frying in a large, deep pan. Drain eggplant (water will make it splatter when it hits the oil, and can be dangerous). When the oil is hot, working in small batches, fry eggplant until lightly browned, then remove to a plate lined with paper towel. Repeat process with plantains and potatoes.

3. In a large pot, heat ½ cup oil (you can use the frying oil), then add sliced onion and sauté, stirring, until golden-translucent.

4. Add ginger, garlic, cloves, cardamom pods, cinnamon stick, curry leaves, pandan leaf (if using), curry powder, cayenne, jaggery, tamarind paste, salt, and ½ cup coconut milk.

5. Gently stir in fried ingredients; add enough water to cover, bring to a boil, cover, and turn down to a simmer. Simmer 10 minutes; vegetables should be cooked through.

6. Remove lid, add remaining coconut milk, stir very gently to combine, taste and adjust seasonings; you may want more salt or a little more tamarind. Simmer 5–10 more minutes, to a thick, rich gravy. Serve hot (or room temperature) with rice; dal is a nice accompaniment to add protein and make a complete meal.

Fried Garlic Curry / Poritha Ulli Kari

(20 minutes, serves 4)

This one is for all the folks who say there can never be too much garlic in a dish. I'm no expert on Ayurvedic cooking, but from what I've read, garlic is used widely in Ayurvedic medicine, with claims that it's good for the heart, hair, and digestive systems.

On the other hand, some practitioners recommend being sparing when you eat garlic and onions, as they can have a 'heating' effect, and some of us may run rather 'hot' already... I leave such weighty health decisions up to the cook! I will only vouch for this dish being delicious.

- 2 Tbsp. vegetable oil
- 2 cups peeled garlic cloves
- 1 cup chopped onion
- 1–3 green chilies, seeded and sliced thinly
- 1 tsp. salt
- ½ tsp. ground pepper
- ½ tsp. fennel seeds
- ¼ tsp. mustard seeds
- ¼ tsp. fenugreek / methi seeds
- 1 stalk curry leaves (about a dozen)
- 2 cups coconut milk
- 1 Tbsp. Sri Lankan roasted curry powder
- 1 Tbsp. tamarind paste

1. Heat oil in a saucepan over medium heat. Add garlic, onions, chilies, salt, pepper, fennel, mustard, fenugreek, and curry leaves; sauté, stirring occasionally, until golden-translucent.

2. Add coconut milk, curry powder, and tamarind paste. Bring to a boil, stirring to combine, then reduce the heat and simmer until the gravy has reduced by half. Serve hot with rice or bread.

Green Chili Curry / Kari-Milaggai Kari

(30 minutes, serves 4)

Green chili curry might sound like it's going to be really spicy, but since we remove the seeds and then add potatoes and coconut milk, the end result of this curry is a pleasant but not overwhelming heat. Pleasant for me, at any rate!

- 6–8 large green chilies (hot or mild, to your taste)
- 1 medium potato, cubed small
- 2 small yellow onions, minced
- 1 Tbsp. vegetable oil
- ½ tsp. fennel seeds
- ½ tsp. fenugreek seeds
- 1 stalk (about a dozen) curry leaves
- 1 cup coconut milk + 1 cup water
- ½ tsp. Sri Lankan curry powder
- ½–1 tsp. salt (to taste)
- 1 tsp. lime juice

1. Remove top end from chilies, slice lengthwise, and removed seeds. (Removing seeds is optional, but if you leave them, the resulting curry will be spicier and possibly a little bitter.)

2. Heat oil in a sauté pan or medium pot on medium-high, add fennel seeds, fenugreek seeds, and curry leaves. Stir for about a minute, until lightly browned.

3. Stir in onions and sauté about five minutes, until onions are golden-brown, stirring occasionally.

4. Stir in potatoes and green chilies, then add curry powder, coconut milk, water, and walt. Bring to a boil, then turn down to simmer.

5. Simmer until potatoes are cooked through; add more water if needed to keep veggies from sticking to the pan.

6. Cook sauce to desired thickness (some like this more liquid, some thicker), and serve hot with rice or bread. (It's also lovely with pittu.)

Green Mango Curry / Maankai Kari

(30 minutes, serves 6)

This dish can be traced as far back as the fifth century, when it was served at the court of King Kasyapa of Sigiriya (famed for his luxurious Sky Palace).

    1 Tbsp. vegetable oil
    3 small onions, minced
    3 cloves garlic, chopped
    1 Tbsp. ginger, chopped
    3 tsp. black mustard seed
    2 stalks curry leaves
    3 green chilies, chopped
    3 Tbsp. vinegar
    3 tsp. Sri Lankan curry powder
    1 tsp. cinnamon
    1 tsp. salt
    3 large green mangoes, peeled and cut into long, thick pieces
    1 can coconut milk
    ½ cup water
    1 Tbsp. sugar

1. Heat the oil in a pan and sauté the onion, garlic, ginger, mustard seeds, curry leaves, and chilies until the onions are soft.

2. Add the vinegar, curry powder, cinnamon, salt, and half a can of coconut milk with ½ cup water—stir to combine.

3. Add the mango slices, bring to a boil, and simmer until the mango is just tender, about ten minutes.

4. Add the rest of the coconut milk and sugar to the curry; bring to a boil, reduce the heat, and simmer for about five minutes. The gravy should be thick enough to thoroughly coat the mango. Serve hot with rice or bread.

Green Jackfruit Curry / Palakkai Kari

(30 minutes, serves 6)

Young jackfruit has a soft and delicate texture and flavor. It's easy to find online in cans, packed in brine; it's also often available at grocery stores, especially ones that cater to vegetarians. If you can find it frozen (often in Indian stores), that will hold up very nicely to cooking, and be much less labor-intensive than working with fresh. This savory curry sauce is delicious served with rice, a green vegetable, and chutneys, pickles, and/or sambols.

Note: For details about how to use ripe jackfruit, see the Ripe Jackfruit Curry recipe.

2 medium onions, chopped fine
1 Tbsp. ginger, chopped fine
3 cloves garlic , chopped fine
3 Tbsp. vegetable oil
¼ tsp. black mustard seed
¼ tsp. cumin seed
1 Tbsp. cayenne
1 tsp. Sri Lankan curry powder
1 lb. young jackfruit, cut into bite-size pieces
⅓ cup ketchup
1 tsp. salt
2 Tbsp. lime juice
1 cup coconut milk + 1 cup water

1. In a large pot, sauté onions, ginger, and garlic in oil on medium-high with mustard seed and cumin seeds until onions are golden / translucent (not brown), stirring as needed. Add cayenne and cook 1 minute, stirring. Immediately stir in curry powder, ketchup, salt, and lime juice.

2. Add jackfruit and stir on high for a few minutes. Add coconut milk and water, stirring gently to combine. Turn down to medium, and let cook 15–20 minutes, stirring occasionally; add water if needed. Serve hot with rice or bread.

Green Tomato and Lentil Curry

(45 minutes, serves 4 as entree, 8 as a side)

Green tomatoes are a lovely end-of-summer curry on their own, beautifully tangy, but add some lentils and you have a complete and nutritious meal. It's perfect with a little rice or bread, or just on its own. In Sri Lanka, earthy red lentils (masoor dal) are most common, and have the advantage of cooking in half the time of most lentils; you could certainly use them in this dish. But I like split mung lentils here; they have a mild, sweet flavor.

Dal:
- 1 cup split mung lentils (moong dal or payatham paruppu)
- ½ tsp. turmeric
- cinnamon stick
- 1 dried red chili, broken into pieces
- 1 cup coconut milk (optional; you can cook in water if preferred)
- 1 cup water (plus more as needed)
- ½ tsp. salt

Green Tomato Curry:
- 1 medium onion, chopped
- 1 tsp. vegetable oil
- 1 tsp. black mustard seeds
- 1 tsp. cumin seed
- 1 tsp. fenugreek seeds
- 1 stalk curry leaves (about a dozen)

5 medium green tomatoes, chopped (about 4 cups)
½ tsp. salt
chopped cilantro to garnish

1. Add 1 cup split mung lentils to a saucepan (with a lid). Add turmeric, cinnamon stick, chili, coconut milk, water, and ½ tsp. salt. Bring to a boil, cover, then turn to medium-low and continue cooking until the lentils are very tender and soft, about 40 minutes. (This can be sped up in a pressure cooker or Instant Pot.) Check periodically and add more water if needed to keep lentils from sticking to the pan. (If they do start to stick, just scrape them up—as long as they don't actually start to burn, they should be fine.)

2. In a separate pot, sauté onion in oil with mustard seed, cumin seed, feungreek seeds, and curry leaves, until onions are golden-translucent.

3. Stir in chopped green tomatoes, cover and turn heat to medium-low; cook 10 minutes.

4. Add the cooked dal to the tomatoes, along with any remaining cooking water. Let the tomatoes and dal come to a boil. Taste, and adjust seasonings to taste—you might add a little more salt, or some lime juice, or more coconut milk.

5. Simmer another 5 minutes, then turn off heat and add chopped cilantro to garnish.

Hibiscus (Shoeflower) Curry / Sembaruthipoo Kari

(45 minutes, serves 6)

In Sri Lanka, hibiscus is commonly known as shoeflower, and is a popular edible flower used in sambols, curries, and beverages. The variety grown there (*rosa sinensis*) is not quite as tangy as *sabdariffa* (the variety most commonly used for hibiscus tea), but has a similar delicate flavor.

Where I live, tropical flowers can only grow in pots. I have a host of them in my sunny windows: jasmine and bougainvillea and hibiscus, mandevilla and duranta. They move out for the summer, then move back inside for the winter. It's perhaps not entirely practical, growing tropicals in Chicagoland, but they speak to something in my heart.

IMPORTANT HEALTH NOTE: Chicago does have hardy hibiscus that grow as perennials outdoors (var. moscheutos and others), but those varieties are less commonly used in cooking. The casual reading I've done on the subject indicates that they are probably also edible, but there are some indications that they may interact with other medications, and there's even one case I ran across of hardy hibiscus acting as an abortifacient. And of course, individuals can have different reactions to different plants.

In general, if you're considering experimenting with plants that aren't established as safely edible, it's recommended that you try very small portions first, checking for negative effects. While I've eaten hardy hibiscus in this preparation and survived, I'd recommend sticking to rosa sinensis for safety. And of course, you'll want to be sure that any flowers you consume were grown for human consumption, without use of pesticides, herbicides, etc.

All that said, this is a dramatic and unusual curry, and could easily be the star of a dinner party. I was introduced to it through Charmaine Solomon's *Complete Asian Cookbook*, and Solomon recommends battering and frying the hibiscus, then simmering it in a curry sauce. That is likely the traditional preparation, but I admit, I don't love it that way—the batter becomes entirely soft. I prefer to drizzle curry sauce over the battered flowers, to retain a little crisp along with the savory softness.

Whichever option you choose, while you can make the curry sauce in advance if you'd like, I'd recommend battering and frying the flowers just before serving, to retain maximum crispness.

Ingredients:
- 12 hibiscus flowers (hibiscus rosa sinensis), traditionally red
- 1 cup flour
- ½ tsp. salt
- 1 measure egg replacer or ½ cup aquafaba, beaten till frothy
- 1 cup cold sparkling water
- oil for deep frying

Curry sauce:
- 1 small onion, finely chopped (about one cup)
- 2 green fingerhot chilies, seeded and chopped
- ¼ tsp. ground turmeric
- one stick cinnamon
- 2 cups coconut milk
- ½ cup water
- 1 tsp. salt
- juice of ½ a lime (about a Tbsp.)

1. Rinse the flowers and blot water with paper towels. Pick off the calyx and stamen. Combine flour, salt, beaten egg replacer or aquafaba, and water to create a smooth batter.

2. Heat oil in a small deep pan. When hot (ideally between 350–375°F), dip each flower in batter, shake off excess, and fry in oil until golden. Remove to paper towels to drain and absorb excess oil.

3. Make curry sauce: Heat 2 Tbsp. vegetable oil in a sauce pan and sauté onions and chilies until golden-translucent. Add turmeric and cinnamon, stir for a minute, than add coconut milk, water, and salt. Bring to a boil, then turn down and simmer.

4. Option 1: add fried hibiscus to the pot and simmer 10 minutes; stir in lime juice, and serve hot with rice.

    Option 2: simmer sauce down on its own for 10 minutes; stir in lime juice. Serve battered hibiscus with rice, with sauce alongside to drizzle over.

Mild Green Plantain Curry

(45 minutes, serves 4)

Green plantains are starchy and not sweet, more like a vegetable than a fruit—if you've had tostones, those are made from green plantains. Expect these fried green plantain bites to be much like potatoes in texture, but with a flavor all their own; I like them simmered in a mild coconut milk curry, with just a hint of green chili.

NOTE: You can save plantain peels to cook them too.

> 3 green plantains (about 4 cups sliced up)
> ½ tsp. salt
> ¼ tsp. turmeric
> oil for deep frying
> ½ red onion, sliced thin
> 2 green finger hot chilies, chopped
> 1 stalk curry leaves, about a dozen
> ¼ tsp. fenugreek seeds
> ½ tsp. salt
> 1 cup coconut milk
> 1 cup water
> 1–2 Tbsp. lime juice

1. Cut plantains in half lengthwise and remove peel with a paring knife. Slice plantains on the diagonal in roughly ¼ inch slices, then toss with ½ tsp. salt and turmeric.

2. Heat oil and fry plantain slices until golden; remove to a plate lined with kitchen towels and set aside.

3. In a separate large sauté pan, heat 1–2 Tbsp. of the oil and add onion, chilies, curry leaves, fenugreek seeds, and salt. Sauté about 10 minutes on medium-high, stirring occasionally, until onions are softened and translucent.

4. Add coconut milk and water, then add fried plantains. Bring to a boil, then turn down heat and simmer 15 minutes, until curry sauce has thickened. Serve hot with rice or bread.

Okra Curry / Vendikkai Kari

(45 minutes, serves 6)

For those afraid of okra, I promise you that this will not be slimy at all. A tender vegetable dish, with a nice toothsome chew to it.

Note: This recipe is a little fussy, because it's designed to make sure the okra is quite dry before cooking—alternatively, you could skip step 2, and add the okra at the end of step 3, before adding curry powder and coconut milk. That would involve just one pan, so easier and faster—about thirty minutes total.

- 1 lb. okra, washed and dried
- ½ tsp. ground turmeric
- ½ tsp. salt
- vegetable oil for frying
- 2 Tbsp. vegetable oil
- 1 onion, sliced thin
- 3 cloves garlic, chopped
- ½ tsp. black mustard seed
- ½ tsp. cumin seed
- ½ tsp. fenugreek seed
- 3–4 dried red chili pods, crumbled
- ½ tsp. Sri Lankan curry powder
- ½ can coconut milk

1. Slice okra thinly on the diagonal, and mix with turmeric and salt.

2. Heat oil in a small frying pan, to deep-fry okra in batches, removing to drain on paper towels. (At this point, okra may be served as is, for a yummy snack.)

3. In a small saucepan, heat oil and sauté onion, garlic, mustard, cumin, fenugreek, and chili pods until onions are soft and golden.

4. Add curry powder and coconut milk; simmer for a few minutes, stirring, until well blended.

5. Add okra to the pot and stir for a few minutes more on low, until well blended. Serve hot with rice.

Pineapple Curry, with Coconut Milk and Saffron

(30 minutes, serves 6)

This is one of the prettiest curries I make, in springtime pink, gold, and green—it's also delicious, sunshine in a bowl. A little sweet, beautifully fruity, creamy with coconut milk, and aromatic with saffron threads. Pairs well with roasted cashews or chickpeas, a green jackfruit curry, or kale mallung.

- 3 Tbsp. vegetable oil
- 1 red onion, chopped fine
- 1 Tbsp. ginger, chopped fine
- 3 garlic cloves, chopped fine
- ¼ tsp. black mustard seed
- ¼ tsp. cumin seed
- 3 green chilies, sliced in half (reduce or skip if desired)
- 1 stalk curry leaves (about a dozen)
- 1 small pineapple, cut into chunks (about 4 cups)
- 1 tsp. salt
- 1 cup coconut milk
- pinch of saffron threads (or ¼ tsp. turmeric)

1. In a large pot, sauté onions, ginger, and garlic in oil on medium-high with mustard seed and cumin seeds until onions are golden/translucent (not brown), stirring as needed.

2. Add green chilies, curry leaves, pineapple, and salt—cook five minutes, stirring occasionally. (Add a little water if needed.)

3. Add coconut milk and saffron threads, stirring gently to combine. Turn down to medium, cover, and let cook 15–20 minutes, stirring occasionally; add water if needed. Serve hot with rice or bread.

Pumpkin Curry

(30–45 minutes, feeds 8)

The orange pumpkins that are so familiar in America don't actually grow in Sri Lanka, but the same approach used for Sri Lankan ash pumpkins (also known as wintermelon) works well for orange pumpkins too, offering a mild, comforting curry rich in autumn flavor.

Typically in Sri Lanka, you'd leave the pumpkin skin on for cooking, and it can then either be eaten, or removed easily with your fingers. But if you're eating with a fork instead of your clean hand, that may be a little tricky to manage—feel free to peel your pumpkin if you like.

One key to this curry is to cut the pumpkin into different sized chunks, so that the smaller pumpkin pieces dissolve into a curry sauce, and the larger ones stay in soft pieces.

I used a medium-sized five pound pumpkin for this dish, but you can certainly reduce the quantity—just reduce the onions and other spices roughly proportionately. But one nice aspect of making a big pumpkin curry, is that after you've eaten it for a day or two, any leftovers can be put on the stove, some broth added, and cooked down into a lovely soup. The soup also freezes well.

¼ cup vegetable oil
5 onions, chopped
3–5 Tbsp. ginger, chopped
5–10 cloves of garlic, chopped
3–5 fresh green or red chilies, chopped (optional)
1 ½ tsp. mustard seed
1 ½ tsp. cumin seed
1 tsp. fenugreek seed
½ tsp. turmeric

- 1 tsp. salt
- 2 stalks curry leaves (about 18–24 leaves)
- 1 medium pumpkin, about five pounds, cut into chunks (peeled if you like)
- 2 cups coconut milk + 2 cups water
- pomegranate and pumpkin seeds for garnish, optional

1. Heat oil in a large pot and sauté onions, ginger, garlic, chilies, and spices over medium heat, stirring, until onions are golden-translucent.

2. Add pumpkin, curry leaves, coconut milk and water; bring to a boil, then turn down to a simmer.

3. Simmer uncovered (adding more water if needed) until the largest pieces of pumpkin are soft and cooked through, about 20–25 minutes. Serve hot with rice or bread, garnished with pomegranate and pumpkin seeds.

Ripe Jackfruit Curry / Palapazham Kari

(1 ½ hours, serves 6)

Jackfruit is enjoying a surge of popularity in the West recently, making it somewhat easier to find fresh jackfruit than previously, though you still may need to venture to an Asian grocery store. You may also be able to find frozen sections there. Do not use canned jackfruit in syrup, as it will be much too sweet.

The trickiest part of this dish is removing the jackfruit pulp from the seeds, fibers, and husk—jackfruit is a little sticky, and oiling your hands beforehand will help. The internet offers many videos showing the process of removing the fruit, which is fairly simple in the end—cut it open, cut out the inedible core, and then separate out the firm fruit, which is similar in appearance to mango, but is more fibrous, and therefore holds up to long cooking.

Once the fruit has been extracted and chopped, and the onions and tomatoes chopped as well, this is an extremely simple one-pot dish, sweet and subtle.

1 lb. fresh ripe jackfruit (yellow fruit), chopped small
1 cup thick coconut milk
½ cup water
2 small onions, minced
1 stalk curry leaves
1 tsp. ground turmeric
1 tsp. cayenne
½ tsp. Sri Lankan curry powder
1 cup tomatoes, chopped

1 Tbsp. tamarind paste
1 2-inch cinnamon stick
1 tsp. salt
juice of ½ a lime (about ½–1 Tbsp.)

1. Combine ingredients in a pot; stir to mix.

2. Bring to a boil, then cover, turn down heat, and simmer for about an hour, until the jackfruit is tender, stirring occasionally. Add water if needed to keep the sauce from burning.

3. Cook down until the fruit is coated in a thick curry sauce. Serve hot with rice and ideally a dry, spicy-salty protein, like crispy chickpeas, for contrast.

Spicy Plantain Curry

(30 minutes, serves 4)

Sri Lanka grows a host of plantains and bananas; this type of curry is typically made with a variety known as ash plantain. That's not easy to find in America, but luckily, plantains generally have become much more available, and they work beautifully in this dish. You can even use very green bananas if you like.

After the first frying stage, the plantains should be just a little bit sweet, and can be eaten straight up if you like as a snack, or added to a plate of rice and curries. But add them to this curry sauce, and the spicy, tangy sauce meets the sweetness of the fried plantain, for what I can only call a taste explosion. In a good way!

NOTE: *You can save plantain or banana peels to cook them too.*

- 3 plantains, peeled (about 4 cups) (or very green bananas)
- ½ tsp. salt
- ¼ tsp. turmeric
- oil for deep frying
- ½ red onion, sliced thin
- 2 green finger hot chilies, chopped
- 1 stalk curry leaves, about a dozen
- ¼ tsp. fenugreek seeds
- 1 tsp. cayenne (or less, adjust to taste)
- ½ tsp. Sri Lankan roasted curry powder
- ½ tsp. salt
- 1 cup coconut milk
- 1–2 Tbsp. lime juice

1. Slice plantains on the diagonal in roughly ¼-inch slices, then toss with ½ tsp. salt and turmeric.

2. Heat oil and fry plantain slices until golden; remove to a plate lined with kitchen towels and set aside.

3. In a separate large sauté pan, heat 1–2 Tbsp. of the oil and add onion, chilies, curry leaves, and fenugreek seeds. Sauté about 10 minutes on medium-high, stirring occasionally, until onions are softened and translucent.

4. Add cayenne, curry powder, and ½ tsp. salt, and stir a few minutes more, then stir in coconut milk.

5. Add fried plantain and lime juice; stir gently to combine. Turn off heat and let sit for 5–10 minutes; the plantains will absorb much of the sauce. Serve hot with rice or bread.

Deviled Potatoes / Urulai Kizhangu

(30 minutes, serves 4)

This was the first vegetable dish I learned to make, and I still find it addictive. It's great with rice and curry, but also works quite well mashed up as a party spread with triangles of toasted naan or pita. For a little more protein, you could add canned and drained chickpeas when you add the potatoes.

- 3 medium onions, chopped
- 3 Tbsp. vegetable oil
- ¼ tsp. black mustard seed
- ¼ tsp. cumin seed
- 1–2 Tbsp. (or more to taste) cayenne
- 3 medium russet potatoes, cubed
- 3 Tbsp. ketchup
- 1 rounded tsp. salt
- ½ cup coconut milk, optional

1. Sauté onions in oil on high with mustard seed and cumin seeds until onions are golden / translucent (not brown). Add cayenne and cook 1 minute. Immediately add potatoes, ketchup, and salt.

2. Lower heat to medium and add enough water so the potatoes don't burn (enough to cover usually works well). Cover and cook, stirring periodically, until potatoes are cooked through, about 20 minutes.

3. Remove lid and simmer off any excess water; the resulting curry sauce should be fairly thick, so that the potatoes are coated with sauce, rather than swimming in liquid. Add coconut milk, if desired, to thicken sauce and mellow spice level; stir until well blended. Serve hot.

Asparagus Poriyal

(15 minutes, serves 4)

This particular recipe is entirely my own invention (though they do make asparagus poriyal in Sri Lanka frequently). I think it came out quite well! A lovely dish for a spring luncheon, with bright green asparagus contrasting beautifully with the chopped red tomato.

- 1 large onion, sliced
- 1 Tbsp. ginger, minced
- 3 cloves garlic, chopped
- 3 green chilies, chopped
- 1 dozen curry leaves (optional)
- 1 tsp. black mustard seed
- 1 tsp. cumin seed
- ½ tsp. fennel seed
- ½ tsp. cayenne
- 1 tsp. salt
- ¼ cup vegetable oil
- 1 lb. asparagus, tough ends removed, cut into pieces
- 1 Tbsp. lime juice
- ½ cup tomatoes, chopped

1. Sauté everything but the asparagus, lime juice, and tomatoes in vegetable oil until onions are transparent (not browned), about five minutes.

2. Add asparagus and lime juice and mix thoroughly; cover and cook five minutes.

3. Remove lid and check asparagus; it should be tender-crisp; sauté a bit more if needed. Stir in tomatoes; cook a few minutes more. Serve hot, with rice and curries.

Brussels Sprouts Poriyal

(20 minutes, serves 4–6)

I never used to like brussels sprouts, but I think it's just that I didn't really know them. Kevin convinced me to try them roasted with olive oil, salt, and pepper, and from there to this was not so far. Now I adore them.

Note: For a fancy appetizer, serve in little glass bowls with tiny forks; a pomegranate seed garnish is a delicious addition, and makes for a holiday festive look; chopped dried cranberries also work!

    2 onions, chopped
    ¼ cup vegetable oil
    ½ thumb-sized piece of ginger, peeled and grated
    3 cloves garlic, minced
    ½ tsp. cumin seed
    ½ tsp. black mustard seed
    1 lb. brussels sprouts
    1 tsp. salt
    ½ tsp. ground turmeric

1. Sauté onions, garlic, and ginger in oil with mustard seeds and cumin seeds until golden. (You can do this on medium, stirring occasionally, while doing the next step, but be careful not to burn them.)

2. Cut ends off brussels sprouts and cut larger pieces in half (or even quarters if they're really huge), so they're all approximately the same size.

3. Microwave sprouts three minutes (this cooks them partway so that they don't take so long on the stovetop that your onions start to burn).

4. Add sprouts to onion mixture, with turmeric and salt. Cook on medium-high, stirring occasionally, until cooked through, about ten minutes.

Cauliflower Poriyal

(25 minutes, serves 4)

The key to this dish is sautéing the cauliflower until it's browned—the browned bits will be the tastiest. This is, oddly, one of my picky children's favorite dishes, and has often proved popular with my friends' children as well. I think it's all the frying.

- 3 medium onions, chopped coarsely
- 3 Tbsp. vegetable oil
- ¼ tsp. black mustard seed
- ¼ tsp. cumin seed
- 1 medium cauliflower, chopped into bite-size pieces
- 1 rounded tsp. salt
- 1 rounded tsp. ground turmeric

1. Sauté onions in oil on high in a large nonstick frying pan with mustard seed and cumin seed, until onions are slightly softened (not brown). Add cauliflower, turmeric, and salt. (I've made this in a regular frying pan, and found that it's difficult not to burn it; if you don't use non-stick, you'll need to stir constantly.)

2. Cook on medium-high, stirring frequently, until cauliflower is browned (mostly yellow, but with a fair bit of brown on the flatter parts). This takes a while—don't stop too early, or it won't be nearly as tasty. Serve hot.

Dried Hibiscus Poriyal

(15–20 minutes, serves 4 as a side)

In Sri Lanka, hibiscus grows freely in many gardens, and it's easy to pick some for a curry. It's a little harder to come by fresh hibiscus blossoms here in Chicagoland, but dried hibiscus is readily available in local Latino markets and online, and coconut milk helps rehydrate the dried blooms.

This poriyal is a bright, tangy element on a rice and curry plate. Be sure to use edible food-grade hibiscus blossoms.

- 2 Tbsp. vegetable oil
- 1 small onion, chopped (about one cup)
- 1 tsp. mustard seed
- 1 tsp. cumin seed
- 1 stalk curry leaves (about a dozen)
- ½ tsp. turmeric
- ½ tsp. salt
- 1 cup dried hibiscus flowers
- ½ cup coconut milk
- 1 cup grated coconut

1. Heat vegetable oil in a medium saucepan and add onion, mustard seed, cumin seed, curry leaves, turmeric, and salt. Sauté on medium high, stirring, until onions are golden-translucent.

2. Add dried hibiscus flowers and stir for a few more minutes until well blended, then add coconut milk and simmer, stirring, for 3–5 minutes more.

3. Stir in fresh grated coconut and serve with rice and curries.

Eggplant, Potato, and Pea Pod Poriyal

(20 minutes, serves 4)

The lush flavor of the eggplant balances well with the soft potatoes and crisp sweetness of the pea pods.

> 2 Japanese eggplants (or one large globe eggplant), diced small
> 1 tsp. salt
> 1 tsp. ground turmeric
> 2 small onions, diced
> ½ cup vegetable oil
> 1 tsp. black mustard seed
> 1 tsp. cumin seed
> 1 dozen curry leaves
> 1 Tbsp. ginger, minced
> 3 cloves garlic, chopped
> 3 small russet potatoes (same volume as eggplant), peeled and diced small
> 3 green chilies, minced
> 1 cup pea pods
> 1 tsp. lime juice

1. Mix eggplant in a bowl with salt and turmeric; set aside.

2. Sauté onions in vegetable oil with mustard seed, cumin seed, curry leaves, ginger, and garlic until golden-translucent.

3. Add potatoes and green chilies, stir occasionally until mostly cooked, about ten minutes.

4. Drain liquid from eggplant (it will have given off some water) and blot dry with paper towels. Add eggplant to pan, mix well, and fry an additional 5–10 minutes.

5. While that's cooking, chop up some pea pods (green beans or sugar snap peas would also work well, or just frozen peas). Add to pan and sauté a few minutes more; stir in lime juice. Serve hot with rice or bread.

Jaffna Whole Eggplant Fry / Yaalpana Kaththarikaii Poriyal

(15–30 minutes, serves 2–4)

Sometimes the simplest dishes are the most fabulous—the base version of this whole eggplant fry uses just a few ingredients (cayenne, turmeric, salt, and hot oil) for delicious and dramatic results. It also dresses up beautifully for a fancier night out, offering grace notes of shallot, green chili, and cherry tomato.

- roughly 1 lb. small eggplants (you can use Indian, Chinese, or other varieties; the key is that they be relatively small)
- 1 Tbsp. cayenne
- 1 tsp. ground turmeric
- 1 tsp. salt
- oil for deep-frying
- 1 large shallot, diced small
- 1 green chili, diced small
- 1 stalk curry leaves, about a dozen
- about a dozen cherry tomatoes, halved
- salt and lime juice to taste
- oil for deep frying

1. Make eight slits down the sides of the eggplants.

2. Mix the cayenne, turmeric, and salt, and rub the spices into the slits (it's fine if they're detached completely at the bottom, which will make it easier to rub in spices).

3. Heat oil for deep frying (around 375°F if using a thermometer) and fry the whole eggplants until they brown evenly, about 3–5 minutes. Remove to a paper towel-lined plate to drain.

   NOTE: You can stop the recipe here and just eat the fried eggplants as is, with rice. Delicious! Or you can add a few more steps for a more complex version.

4. To a sauté pan, add a few Tbsp. of the oil from deep frying, and add diced shallot, diced chili, curry leaves, and tomatoes. Cook on medium-high, stirring, about 5 minutes, until onions are golden-translucent and tomatoes have softened.

5. Add whole fried eggplant to pan and cook an additional 5–10 minutes, stirring; taste and adjust seasonings—you may want to add ½ tsp. salt, or up to a tablespoon of lime juice at this point. Serve hot with rice, and enjoy!

Mixed Vegetable Poriyal

(20 minutes, serves 4)

This one is super-convenient, since you can keep the frozen veggies in your freezer and it thus doesn't require going to the grocery store, as long as you already have onions. And if you don't already have onions, well, you're going to have trouble cooking these dishes, is all I can say. I've included two variations that work well, using fresh vegetables, but there are many other possibilities. This is one of the first dishes I learned to cook, and I made it often during grad school.

- 3 medium onions, chopped
- 3 Tbsp. vegetable oil
- ¼ tsp. black mustard seed
- ¼ tsp. cumin seed
- 1 large package frozen mixed vegetables, thawed and drained, bite-size pieces
- 1 rounded tsp. salt
- 1 rounded tsp. ground turmeric

1. Sauté onions in oil on high with mustard seed and cumin seeds until onions are golden / translucent (not brown). Add mixed vegetables, turmeric, and salt.

2. Cook on medium-high, stirring periodically, until vegetables are cooked through and almost dry. Serve hot with rice or bread.

Note: The variation below using fresh vegetables will take longer, since you need to add in prep time, and since potatoes take longer to cook.

Variation: Potatoes, Peas, and Tomatoes:

1. In a large frying pan, sauté chopped onions in oil on high with mustard seed, cumin seeds, and curry leaves; cook until onions are golden / translucent. Add chopped and peeled russet potatoes, turmeric, and salt. Mix well.

2. Cook on medium-high, stirring occasionally, until potatoes are mostly cooked through and starting to stick. Add chopped tomatoes and continue to stir. When tomatoes are well-reduced, add peas and continue to stir. Cook until peas have lost their bright green color and much of their moisture; the ingredients should be well blended in flavor, and the potatoes should be somewhat browned. Serve hot with rice or bread.

Tempered Lentils / Paruppu

(1 hour, serves 6)

Lentils are a staple dish in Sri Lanka—across the country, people eat what we call paruppu daily, at breakfast, lunch, and dinner. It's terribly good for you, very affordable, and also delicious. I used to dislike lentils, or I thought I did, but it turned out I only disliked my mother's version (which everyone else loved, so I blame my being a slightly picky kid). I was converted to lentils through my adult discovery of Ethiopian food, a cuisine which cooks the lentils to a soft porridge-like consistency; now I am quite fond of them. This recipe is adapted from Charmaine Solomon's *The Complete Asian Cookbook*.

> 2 cups red lentils
> 1 can coconut milk, plus 1 can hot water
> 1 dried red chili, broken into pieces
> 1 pinch of ground saffron
> 2 Tbsp. vegetable oil
> 2 medium onions, finely sliced
> 6 curry leaves
> 1 2-inch cinnamon stick
> 3 strips of lemon rind (about a quarter lemon)
> ¾ –1 tsp. salt (to taste)

1. Put lentils in a saucepan with the coconut milk, chili, and saffron. (If you don't have red lentils, you can use a different variety, but it will notably change the flavor.) Fill the can with hot water and add that as well; this will ensure you don't waste any coconut yumminess. Bring to a boil, then cover and simmer until lentils are

soft, about forty-five minutes. Stir periodically and add more water if needed; it's fine if the bottom starts to stick a little—just scrape it up.

2. In another saucepan, heat the oil and fry the onions, curry leaves, cinnamon, and lemon rind until onions are golden-brown.

3. Reserve half the onions for garnishing the dish and add the lentil mixture to the saucepan. Stir well, add salt to taste, and cook down until thick, like porridge. Serve with rice and curries.

Note: Some people like their paruppu more watery, but I think they're just wrong. Still, cook to your preference.

Tempered Potatoes

(20 minutes, serves 4)

imple, classic—my kids love this preparation.

    3 russet potatoes, peeled
    1 onion, sliced
    3–4 cloves garlic, sliced
    3 Tbsp. lime juice
    1–2 tsp. dried red chili pieces
    ½ tsp. cayenne
    ¼ tsp. ground turmeric
    ¼ cup vegetable oil
    1 ½ tsp. black mustard seed
    1 2-inch cinnamon stick
    1 dozen curry leaves
    1 tsp. salt

1. Boil potatoes, drain, and cut into large chunks or small dice, as you prefer.

2. In a medium bowl, mix these ingredients: onion, garlic, lime juice, chili pieces, cayenne, turmeric, and salt.

3. Heat oil in a saucepan on medium heat; when oil is ready add mustard seeds and let it pop up (nearly 2–4 seconds). Then add cinnamon and curry leaves and let it fry for 1–2 minutes. Then add the onion mixture and stir to mix.

4. Turn heat to medium, and fry, stirring occasionally, until onions are translucent-golden, about 10 minutes; be careful not to burn them. The mixture should be very aromatic by this stage.

5. Add potatoes into the onion mixture, mixing well, but don't break the potatoes into small pieces. Stir for a minute or two until well blended; taste and add salt and/or lime juice as desired. Serve with rice or bread.

Broccoli Varai

(30 minutes, serves 4)

 good way to get green vegetables into children.

Note: I keep this fairly mild, so my kids will eat it, but for a spicier (and more traditional) version, chop 2–3 green chilies, and stir them in during step 1.

> 1 lb. broccoli (crowns and/or stalks), chopped fine (by hand or in food processor)
> 1 medium onion, chopped fine
> 1–2 Tbsp. vegetable oil
> 6–12 curry leaves
> 1 1-inch cinnamon stick
> ¼ tsp. black mustard seed
> ¼ tsp. cumin seed
> 1 tsp. black pepper (or cayenne)
> 1 tsp. salt
> ½ tsp. ground turmeric
> ½ cup shredded unsweetened coconut
> 2 Tbsp. oil (optional)
> 1 tsp. sugar (optional)
> 1–2 tsp. lime juice (optional)

1. Sauté onions in oil on high with curry leaves, cinnamon, mustard seeds, and cumin seeds until onions are golden / translucent (not brown).

2. Add broccoli, salt, pepper, and turmeric; fry, stirring, for a few minutes. (If the broccoli starts sticking to the bottom of the pan, you can add a little water.)

3. Add in coconut and stir for five minutes.

4. Taste, and stir in sugar and/or lime juice if desired. Serve hot, with rice and curries.

Cabbage Varai / Muttaikoss Varai

(15–20 minutes, serves 8)

weet, firm, rich with coconut.

> 8 oz. cabbage
> 1 medium onion, minced
> 2 fresh green chilies, seeded and chopped
> ¼ rounded tsp. ground turmeric
> ¼ rounded tsp. freshly ground black pepper
> 1 rounded tsp. salt
> ½ cup shredded unsweetened coconut

1. Shred cabbage finely. Wash well, drain, and put into a large saucepan. Don't worry about drying the water clinging to the cabbage—you actually want that water to help steam the cabbage.

2. Add all the other ingredients except the coconut. Cover and cook gently until cabbage is tender, stirring periodically.

3. Uncover, add coconut, stir well, and when the liquid in the pan has been absorbed by the coconut, remove from heat. Allow to cool before serving.

Green Bean Varai

(15–20 minutes, serves 8)

 A fresh, green element on the dinner plate.

    1 medium onion, minced
    1 tsp. black mustard seed
    ¼ rounded tsp. ground turmeric
    1–3 dried red chilies, broken into pieces (optional)
    1 lb. green beans, chopped fine (in a food processor is fine)
    ¼ rounded tsp. freshly ground black pepper
    1 rounded tsp. salt
    ½ cup shredded unsweetened coconut

1. Cook onions with turmeric, black mustard seed, and chilies in a dry pan over high heat, stirring constantly, for a few minutes, until slightly softened.

2. Add green beans, pepper, and salt, and cook a few minutes more, enough to take the raw edge off. Green beans should still be crispy.

3. Turn off heat, stir in coconut, and serve with rice.

Lime-Masala Mushrooms

(20 minutes, serves 4)

Another one of my own invention; quick and easy to make. Rich in flavor, a favorite of hobbits and my dinner guests. This one is easy to start going and then just stir every once in a while as it cooks, so it's convenient for a dinner party when you have twelve things going at once

- 1 ½ lbs. mushrooms, sliced or quartered
- 1 stick salted vegan butter
- ½ rounded tsp. salt, or to taste
- 1 tsp. black pepper
- 1 tsp. Sri Lankan curry powder
- ¼ cup lime juice, or to taste

1. Sauté mushrooms in vegan butter and salt and cook on high heat until quite reduced, stirring frequently.

2. Add curry powder, pepper, and lime juice and cook until juice is absorbed. Mushrooms should be glistening and slightly fried, not sitting in liquid. Serve hot with rice and curries. (Also nice on toast.)

Marinated Ginger-Garlic Tofu

(with Seitan and Tempeh Variations)

(20 minutes plus marinating time, serves 2–4)

This is definitely a fusion dish—I combined our Sri Lankan ginger-garlic spicing with a traditional marinated tofu recipe, for a result that I found delectably more-ish. I didn't even wait to make rice, but just kept nibbling pieces right off of the serving plate. Yum!

> 8 oz. extra-firm tofu, cubed small
> ½ tsp. garlic powder
> ½ tsp. ginger powder
> ½ tsp. turmeric
> ½ tsp. salt
> ½–1 tsp. cayenne
> 1 Tbsp. lime juice plus more to garnish
> 2 Tbsp. oil
> oil to fry
> 2 shallots, sliced
> sesame seeds, chopped chives, chopped cilantro to garnish

1. Combine tofu, spices, 1 Tbsp. lime juice and 2 Tbsp. oil in a bowl and stir gently to combine. Marinate for 20–30 minutes (or longer, if you like), for additional flavor.

2. Heat oil in a sauté pan and pan-fry on high, stirring, for about 5 minutes. (You may deep-free or bake, if preferred. If you deep-fry,

you'll likely get more textural contrast between the crispy outer tofu and the soft interior.) Remove to a plate lined with paper towel to drain excess oil.

NOTE: You can stop and eat it at this stage, but it will be even tastier if you continue...

3. In the same pan, sauté sliced shallots on medium-high (adding oil if needed), stirring, until golden-brown and slightly crispy.

4. In serving bowl / plate, top tofu with shallots, then garnish with another 1–2 Tbsp. of lime juice (to your taste), a little white sesame seed, chives, and cilantro. Chopped cashews would also be nice as a garnish. Serve hot with rice.

SEITAN VARIATION

(10 minutes plus marinating time, serves 2–4)

Seitan is wheat gluten, made by washing wheat flour dough with water until all the starch granules have been removed, leaving only the gluten. The resulting mass can then be cut into small pieces, which expand on cooking.

An easy and satisfying weeknight dish; I recommend trying it with rice and an eggplant or mango curry.

> 8 oz. seitan
> ½ tsp. garlic powder
> ½ tsp. ginger powder
> ½ tsp. turmeric
> ½ tsp. salt
> ½–1 tsp. black pepper (or cayenne, if you'd like it spicier)

    1 Tbsp. lime juice
    2 Tbsp. oil
    ¼ cup besan / chickpea flour (or wheat flour)
    oil to fry

1. Combine seitan, spices, lime juice and 2 Tbsp. oil in a bowl and stir gently to combine. Seitan will break up into small pieces as you stir. Marinate for 20–30 minutes (or longer, if you like), for additional flavor.

2. Toss gently in flour.

3. Heat oil in a sauté pan and pan-fry on high, stirring, for about 5 minutes. Remove to a plate lined with paper towel to drain excess oil. Serve hot with rice or naan and a vegetable curry or sambol.

NOTE: Seitan can be made easily from scratch, if you'd prefer to buying it ready-made.

TEMPEH VARIATION

(10 minutes plus marinating time, serves 2–4)

Tempeh is a traditional Javanese soy product that is made from fermented soybeans, with a distinctive texture and flavor. Personally, I can enjoy a little bit of this—I'd like it tossed in a salad, for example, but don't necessarily want a lot of it straight up as an entree.

    8 oz. tempeh, cubed small
    ½ tsp. garlic powder
    ½ tsp. ginger powder
    ½ tsp. turmeric
    ½ tsp. salt

1 tsp. jaggery or brown sugar
1 Tbsp. lime juice
2 Tbsp. oil plus oil to fry

1. Combine tempeh, spices, lime juice and 2 Tbsp. oil in a bowl and stir gently to combine. Marinate for 20–30 minutes (or longer, if you like), for additional flavor.

2. Heat oil in a sauté pan and pan-fry on high, stirring, for about 5 minutes. (If you prefer, you can either deep-fry or bake the tempeh.) Remove to a plate lined with paper towel to drain excess oil. Serve hot.

Roasted Brussels Sprouts with Jaggery, Balsamic, and Cayenne

(35 minutes, serves 2–4)

I love roasting brussels sprouts on a weeknight—five minutes of prep and the rest happens in the oven (or toaster oven, in my case), giving you plenty of time to cook a few more dishes.

These brussels sprouts are sweet, tangy, and a little spicy. A nice addition to the Thanksgiving table, or for dinner any night of the week.

- 1 lb. brussels sprouts
- 3 Tbsp. jaggery or dark brown sugar
- 3 cloves garlic, minced
- 3 Tbsp. balsamic vinegar
- 3 Tbsp. olive oil
- ¼ tsp. salt (plus more to sprinkle)
- ½ tsp. cayenne

1. Preheat oven to 400°F.

2. Trim and halve brussels sprouts, cutting large sprouts smaller, aiming to have them roughly the same size so they'll cook evenly.

3. In a bowl, mix together jaggery, garlic, balsamic, oil, salt, and cayenne. Add sprouts and stir to coat them well.

4. Line a baking sheet with foil or parchment paper; spread brussels sprouts in a single layer.

5. Roast for 25–30 minutes; taste and sprinkle on additional salt as desired to finish (I like another ¼ tsp. or so).

Vegetable and Lentil Stew / Sambar

(45 minutes, serves 8)

This vegetable-lentil stew is a very malleable dish—make it with whichever vegetables please you, though pumpkin, okra, eggplant, drumsticks, and tomatoes are traditional. You can also vary the types of lentils used, and the spice level—some people leave the chili and pepper out entirely, some make it quite spicy. This version is somewhere in between, and makes for a healthy protein-packed breakfast or light dinner served with idli, thosai, or rice, and a little coconut chutney.

If you need it ready in a hurry, you can prepare sambar in a pressure cooker, just throwing everything in, but if you do it in stages as below, you'll get more richness of flavor.

Note: I don't recommend using potato if you plan to freeze some of it, as the potato will turn mealy on freezing. Otherwise, sambar generally freezes well.

2 small Japanese eggplants or one large globe eggplant, cubed
1 tsp. salt
1 tsp. ground turmeric
½ cup red lentils (masoor dal)
2 cups pumpkin (or winter squash)
2 carrots
1 drumstick, cut into 3-inch pieces
1 red onion, diced
1 Tbsp. ginger, minced
3 cloves garlic, chopped
4–6 cups water, as needed to cover vegetables

1 cup green beans, chopped
1 cup tomato, chopped
1 tsp. tamarind paste
1 tsp. salt
1 tsp. black pepper
2 Tbsp. sambar powder
1 ½ Tbsp. oil
6–8 okra, sliced
2 cups mushrooms, quartered

For tempering:
1 ½ Tbsp. oil
½ tsp. black mustard seed
½ tsp. split urad dal (black gram / matpe bean / ulunththu)
2 dried red chilies
1 stalk curry leaves

1. In a medium bowl, mix eggplant with salt and turmeric and set aside. (This draws the bitterness out of the eggplant.)

2. Put dal, pumpkin, carrots, drumstick, onion, ginger, garlic, and water in a large pot and bring to a boil; turn to medium-high and let cook about ten minutes, stirring periodically. If the water boils off too much, add more—you're aiming for a watery stew / thick soup in the end.

3. Add green beans, tomato, tamarind paste, salt, black pepper, and sambar powder; cook another ten minutes.

4. While sambar is cooking, in a separate frying pan, heat oil, then add okra and fry for a few minutes, stirring. Add mushrooms and continue to stir.

5. Drain any water from eggplant, blotting with a paper towel, and then add eggplant to pan and fry for a few minutes more. Add okra,

mushrooms, and eggplant to the large pot of sambar, and continue to simmer, adding water if needed.

6. Tempering stage: heat remaining oil in the same frying pan on medium-low; add mustard seeds and urad dal and sauté, stirring, for a few minutes, until seeds begin to pop and dal turns a dark reddish-brown. Add dry chilies and curry leaves; sauté until the leaves become crisp and the chilies have darkened.

7. Stir in tempered seasonings to the pot of sambar, adding water if needed to desired thickness. Taste and add salt if needed. Serve hot, with idli, thosai, or rice.

Mambalam, nala mambalam,
Mama than tha mambalam,
Munjel vunai mambalam,
Munum vesum mambalam.

Mango, nice mango,
Uncle gave me a mango,
It is a yellow mango,
A sweet-smelling mango.

—*Tamil children's rhyme*

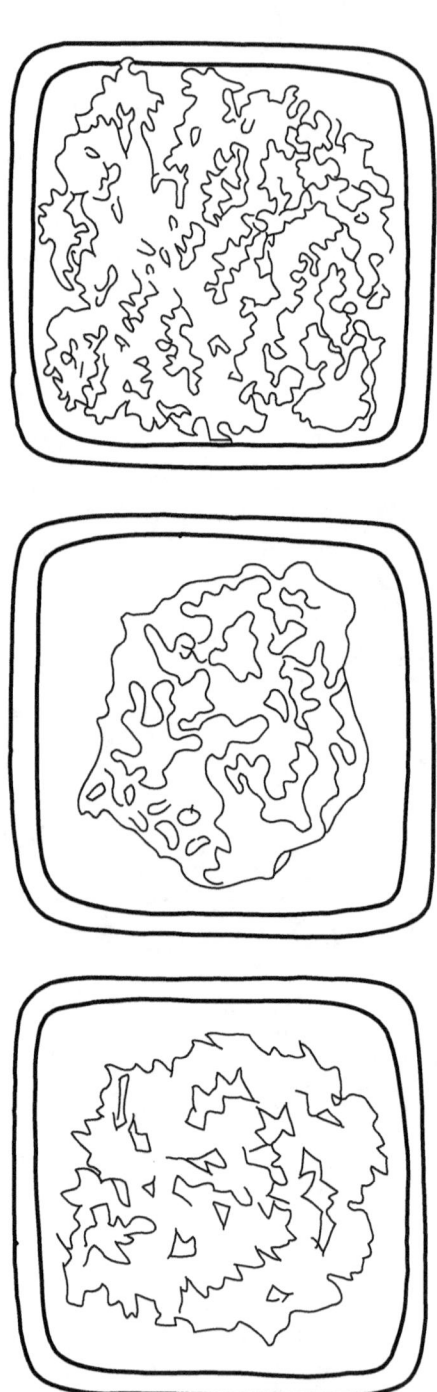

ACCOMPANIMENTS, SALDS, and SNACKS

FRIED SNACKS

Bonda
Chili-Mango Cashews / Kari-Maankai Kaju
Lentil Patties / Kadalai Vadai
Stir-Fried Chickpea Snack / Kadalai Sundal
Vegetable Cutlets

SALADS

Cucumber Salad
Pickled Beet Salad
Rose (or Hibiscus) Salad / Rosappu Pachadi

CHUTNEYS

Cranberry-Rhubarb Chutney
Green Coconut Chutney / Thengai Chutney
Green Tomato Chutney with Apples
Mango-Ginger Chutney

SAMBOLS

Bitter Gourd Sambol / Paavakkai Sambol
Chili Onion Sambol / Lunu Miris Sambol
Coconut Sambol / Thengai-Poo, or Pol Sambol
Eggplant Sambol / Kaththarikkai Sambol
Ginger Sambol / Injii Sambol
Kale Sambol

Plantain Sambol
Rose Sambol
Sweet Onion Sambol / Seeni Sambol

PICKLES

Eggplant Pickle / Brinjal Moju
Lime Pickle
Mango Pickle / Maankai Oorukkai
Quick-Pickled Cucumber-Carrot Relish
Spicy Pineapple Pickle / Achar

SPECIAL DISHES

Cucumber-Tomato Raita
Leeks Fried with Chili
Spiced Tomato Jam / Thakkaali Yaam

ACCOMPANIMENTS, SALADS, *and* SNACKS

If you're short on time, rice and a vegetable is a sufficient Sri Lankan meal—but traditionally, you would also enjoy at least one or two accompaniments: sambols, chutneys, pickles, salads, and more. They tend to be intensely flavored, and bring balance and excitement to a plate, making it possible for everyone at the table to balance the meal to their own tastes, adding a little sweetness, chili heat, bitter tang, and more.

Sambols and salads can be cooked very quickly. Once you put the rice on, you still usually have time to make one or two of these while the rice is cooking. Others, such as chutneys and pickles, are best made in advance, and will keep for a long time in the fridge (or store unopened in the pantry, if properly sealed). They serve quite a few people—each person is meant to just take a little bit.

Of course, you can't guarantee that people will hold to that! Many of my friends tend to treat coconut sambol like a vegetable and just pile it on their plate. You can do that too, if you like, remembering that coconut is full of rich, fatty goodness.

Oh, and if you or your friends find spicy heat challenging, some cucumber-tomato raita is an essential palate-cooler. A glass of your favorite non-dairy milk or mango lassi also helps. Remember—water only spreads the fire.

Bonda

(45 minutes, serves 4)

This is a crispy chickpea batter snack, filled with fluffy, light seasoned potatoes, commonly sold by street vendors and packed in tiffin containers. You can serve bondas with any chutney you like—cilantro, coconut, mint, tamarind, tomato, etc. Best eaten while still hot!

Filling:
- 2 medium potatoes (about 1 lb.)
- ½ tsp. black mustard seed
- 2 dried red chilies, broken into pieces
- 2 small onions, finely chopped (about 2 cups)
- 1 small green chili, finely chopped
- 2 stalks fresh curry leaves
- ½ tsp. fine salt
- 1 cup water
- ½ tsp. lime juice
- 2 Tbsp. vegetable oil

Batter:
- 1 cup chickpea flour
- 2 Tbsp. rice flour
- 2 pinches baking soda
- ½ tsp. fine salt
- ¼ tsp. ground turmeric
- 1 cup warm water
- additional vegetable oil for deep-frying

1. Boil potatoes until cooked through, drain and let cool. Peel and mash the potatoes.

2. Heat 2 Tbsp. oil in a sauté pan over medium-high heat; add mustard seeds and dried chilies; fry for a minute. Then add onion and green chili, turn down to medium and cook, stirring as needed, until onion is golden-translucent.

3. Add the mashed potato, curry leaves, ½ tsp. salt, 1 cup water, ½ tsp. lime juice. Cook, stirring periodically, until water is absorbed and the mixture is thick.

4. Remove pan from heat, remove any large pieces of dried chili and any large curry leaves. Taste and adjust seasoning as desired, let cool, and refrigerate until firm. Shape the mixture into small balls. (The balls of seasoned potato can be wrapped in plastic wrap and refrigerated for a few days if desired.)

5. Make batter: combine ingredients and whisk until well-blended.

6. Heat oil for deep-frying (to about 375°F if you have a food thermometer). Dip the potato balls in to the batter, then deep-fry for a few minutes, until golden. Remove to a paper-towel-lined plate to drain, and serve warm, with chutney.

Chili-Mango Cashews / Kari-Maangai Kaaju

(10 minutes + drying time, makes 12 servings)

2 cups dried mango slices, chopped (kitchen shears or food processor recommended)
2 cups roasted, salted cashews, chopped
1–2 Tbsp. vegan butter
1-2 tsp. cayenne
1 tsp. Sri Lankan curry powder
1–2 tsp. crumbled jaggery or brown sugar
enough water to make a glaze
salt or sugar to taste

1. Line a flat cookie sheet or tray with foil; set aside.

2. In a dry pan on medium-high, toast cashews for a few minutes, stirring, until nuts smell yummy.

3. Add vegan butter, cayenne, curry powder, sugar / jaggery, and some water to make a thin glaze. Turn down to medium, and stir for a few minutes until nuts are nicely coated and cooked. (Stir continuously, or nuts will burn.)

4. Stir in mango bits until well combined. Taste (carefully, as it will be hot!), add salt / sugar as desired.

5. Spread flat on foil-lined tray to cool.

Lentil Patties / Kadalai Vadai

(45 minutes, plus 2 hours lentil soaking time, makes about 24–30)

When you go visiting in Sri Lanka, your hosts will often insist on quickly frying up some vadai for you, accompanied by hot, sweet tea. You can protest once, for politeness's sake, that they shouldn't go to the trouble. Then say yes.

Vadai typically don't refrigerate and reheat well; they're best served hot, right after frying, but are also tasty at room temperature. Vadai are a perfect mid-afternoon snack with tea or coffee or mango-passionfruit juice; they also make a terrific picnic or road-trip food.

> 1 cup split red lentils / masoor dal
> 1 large onion, chopped
> 3 green chilies, chopped
> 3 dried red chilies, broken into small pieces
> 1 Tbsp. ginger, minced
> 3 garlic cloves
> 1 dozen curry leaves
> 1 tsp. cumin seeds
> 1 tsp. fennel seeds
> 1 tsp. salt
> oil for deep frying
> rice flour if needed

1. Soak lentils for at least two hours. (Can be done overnight.) Drain.

    NOTE: Typically, people often prefer a coarser texture to their vadai—for that, set aside half the lentils and/or the chopped onions before the next step, and just mix them back in after grinding, to preserve more texture. I'm a bit of an outlier that I like my vadai to be more finely-textured.

2. Add the lentils to food processor with other ingredients; grind coarsely, scraping down the sides with a rubber spatula once or twice so they're well blended.

3. Set oil to heating. While it heats, mold the mixture into small balls (if the dough is too wet to mold, add rice flour 1–2 tablespoon at a time, until it reaches a workable texture). Flatten them into patties.

4. Gently slip into the hot oil and deep fry both sides, until crisp and golden brown.

5. Remove with slotted spoon and drain on paper towel. Serve hot or at room temperature; they can be eaten straight up, but I like to add a little mint-cilantro chutney or mango pickle. They're also commonly served with other chutneys, pickles, sambar, or vegan yogurt.

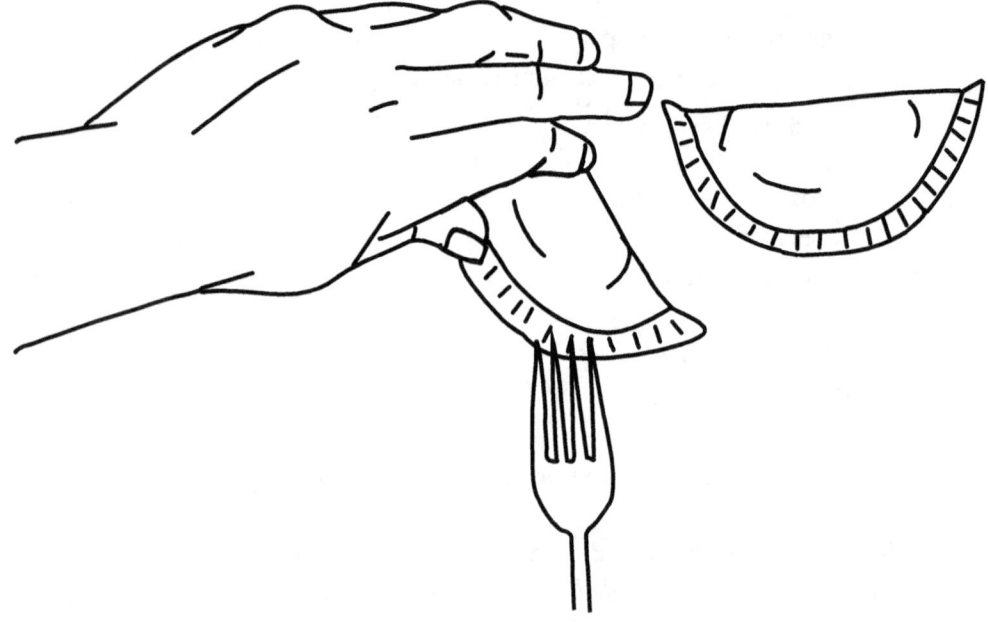

Stir-fried Chickpea Snack / Kadalai Sundal

(90 minutes + soaking time, serves 4–8)

Sundals are savory snacks; this one is popular served in a newspaper cone, to be nibbled at while strolling on a sunny beach. Fluffy seasoned chickpeas offer healthy nutrition, but more importantly, they're delicious!

> 2 cups dried chickpeas, soaked overnight (or 4 15-oz. cans)
> 2–3 Tbsp. vegetable oil
> 8–10 red pearl onions (or 2–3 large shallots), sliced finely
> 3–5 dried red chilies, broken into pieces
> ½ tsp. cayenne
> 1 tsp. salt
> 1 Tbsp. lime juice
> 1 cup green mango, chopped

1. Drain chickpeas and rinse in cold water.

2. Heat oil in a large pot on medium-high; add onions (or shallots) and chilies; sauté stirring until onions are translucent.

3. Add chickpeas, cayenne, and salt to the same pot, with sufficient water to cover. Bring to a boil, then turn down and cook until tender, approximately 1 hr. Near the end of cooking, remove lid and let any remaining water boil off; for the final result, chickpeas should be glistening with a light sheen of oil.

4. Remove from heat and stir in lime juice and chopped mango; mix thoroughly and serve as a snack, or as an accompaniment to a rice and curry meal.

   NOTE: Common variations include sautéing mustard seeds, curry leaves, and/or chopped green chili with the onions, and stirring in fresh coconut and/or chopped raw onion at the end.

Vegetable Cutlets

(90 minutes, makes about 50)

There's a part of my mind (formed in childhood over monthly Sri Lankan birthday parties at various aunties' homes) that says a party isn't properly a party unless there are cutlets. So when people agree to come over to my house and let me feed them cutlets, it makes that childhood bit of me very happy.

- 1 lb. mixed vegetables, diced small (frozen mixed veg. works fine, just thaw it first)
- 2 large russet potatoes
- 4 medium onions, chopped fine, for sautéing
- 1 tsp. black mustard seed
- 1 tsp. cumin seed
- 2 Tbsp. oil
- 1 rounded tsp. salt
- ⅔ cup lime juice
- 2 small onions, minced, for mixing in
- 4 rounded tsp. fresh green chilies, chopped fine
- 1 rounded tsp. ground black pepper
- a few tsp. chickpea flour (or other flour) mixed with water to make a paste, for dipping
- dry breadcrumbs, for coating
- oil for deep frying

1. Boil the potatoes, peel, and mash them.

2. Sauté the four fine-chopped medium onions in oil with cumin and black mustard seed until golden-translucent. Add vegetables, salt and lime juice, then cook until very dry. Let cool.

3. Using your clean hand, mix thoroughly the vegetable mixture, mashed potatoes, the two small minced raw onions, black pepper, and chilies until a fairly smooth paste. Taste and add up to ½ tsp. more fine salt if desired.

4. Shape the mixture into small balls, about the size of a cupped palm. I squeeze the mixture in my balled hand as I go, compressing so the resulting ball is nice and firm—that helps it keep its form when frying. (You can pause, cover with plastic wrap, and refrigerate at this point if making a day or two ahead.)

5. Mix chickpea flour with enough water to make a thin, watery paste. Roll each ball in the flour-water mixture, and then roll each ball in the dry breadcrumbs. (You can freeze at this point if making ahead—spread them out on a flat cookie sheet so they're not touching and freeze them—once frozen, you can pack them more tightly in gallon ziploc bags, and they should hold their shape. They'll be fine in the freezer for weeks, which helps when you're prepping for a big party; you can either fry them frozen or spread them out on plates and let them thaw first.)

6. Fry a few at a time in deep hot oil over medium-high heat—not too hot, or they'll start to break apart! This should take a minute or so each. When well-browned, lift out with a slotted spoon and drain on a metal rack placed over a tray lined with a few layers of paper towels.

Cucumber Salad

(5 minutes, serves 8)

 cool, refreshing bite, slightly crisp.

> 1 English cucumber (or 2 Persian cucumbers), sliced into bite-size pieces
> ½ cup thinly sliced onion
> 1 green chili, chopped fine
> ¼ tsp. salt
> ¼ tsp. freshly ground black pepper
> ¼ tsp. sugar
> 1 Tbsp. lime juice or rice vinegar
> 2 Tbsp. coconut milk

1. Combine and serve with rice or uppuma and curry, with perhaps a nice mango pickle on the side.

Pickled Beet Salad

(30 minutes, serves 8)

 A sweet-sour accompaniment that can be eaten fresh; the flavors will mellow and blend if allowed to sit for a few days.

Note: Half a red onion, sliced and added at step 3, would grace this dish nicely.

> 2 cups raw beet, peeled, cut in half, and sliced
> 4 tsp. cumin seeds
> 1 tsp. salt
> ¼ cup sugar
> 1 cup vinegar

1. In a saucepan, boil beets in water; cook until beets are tender, about 10–15 minutes.

2. Sauté cumin seeds in a dry pan for a few minutes, stirring, until they start to smell fragrant. Remove from heat.

3. Drain beets, return to saucepan, combine with remaining ingredients and cumin seeds, bring to a boil, and simmer 10–15 minutes.

4. You can now cool and serve immediately with rice and curries, or alternatively, let cool, pour beets and liquid into a jar, close, and refrigerate. Eat within a few weeks (unless you follow proper procedures for long-term canning).

Rose (or Hibiscus) Salad / Rosappu Pachadi

(15 minutes, serves 4)

This is an ancient recipe, based primarily on a recipe N. Maheswari Devi saved from 13th–14th century manuscripts in the Jaffna Library. The library, which contained over 97,000 books and manuscripts and was one of the largest in Asia, was burned by an organized mob on June 1, 1981, during the Sri Lankan conflict, one of the great tragedies of that era. The burning was one of the most violent examples of ethnic biblioclasm of the 20th century.

Although the library has since been rebuilt, many irreplaceable manuscripts were lost to the world. I offer this recipe to you with gratitude to the author for her work researching and saving many such recipes, and recommend her book to you, *Jaffna Heritage Cooking*.

Roses bloom lushly in the hill country of Sri Lanka; if roses aren't available, hibiscus (shoeflower) also works beautifully here, lending a little more tang. You can prepare this recipe either as a lightly-dressed salad, or as more of a vegan yogurt-based raita, a cooling element with a spicy curry meal.

Petals are quite perishable, so this should be made and served fresh for a salad; a raita will keep for a few days in the fridge.

NOTE: It's important to only eat flowers that haven't been treated with pesticides or other poisons when cooking; if you're not growing the flowers yourself, be sure to buy from reputable sources that certify they are food-grade quality.

about 40 rosebuds, or 20 roses
3–5 green chilies, minced
½ cup fresh grated coconut
½ cup red onion, minced
¼–1 cup vegan yogurt (determine amount depending on whether you're aiming for a dressed salad, as pictured, or something closer to a raita)
1 tsp. fresh mint, minced
½ tsp. salt

1. If using rosebuds, remove the petals from the base. If using fully-grown roses, tear or chop the petals small (otherwise, the large petals will have an unappetizing slick texture). Rinse and drain them well before continuing.

2. Combine petals with remaining ingredients, stirring to mix well. Serve cold.

Cranberry-Rhubarb Chutney

(20–25 minutes, makes 1 quart)

Kevin loves both cranberries and rhubarb, so I decided to combine them, just for him. You can enjoy this chutney right away, or put it up and save it to pull out at the holidays. Festive! As with any chutney, adjust to your taste—you can make it a little sweeter, a little tangier, a little spicier.

NOTE: Rhubarb leaves are toxic and humans should never ingest them. Please resist the urge to save them for a salad.

> 1 red onion, chopped fine
> 2 Tbsp. chopped ginger
> 1 cup apple cider vinegar
> about 2 cups cranberries
> 1 cup chopped dates or golden raisin
> zest of one lime
> 1 stick cinnamon
> ½ tsp. crushed red pepper flakes
> 2 Tbsp. jaggery or dark brown sugar (or more to taste)
> about 1 cup chopped rhubarb stalks

1. Combine all ingredients except rhubarb in a medium pot, bring to a boil, then turn down heat and simmer 10–20 minutes, stirring occasionally, until cranberries have popped and you have a sauce-like consistency.

2. Add rhubarb (if you add it at the beginning, it'll lose all definition) and cook an additional 5 minutes, stirring. Rhubarb should be soft and cooked through.

3. Serve room temperature; chutney is a fabulous sandwich spread. Will keep for two weeks in the fridge, or may be canned for long-term storage.

Green Coconut Chutney / Thengai Chutney

(10 minutes, serves 8)

This accompaniment adds a fresh, tangy element to a South Asian meal. If you'd like it to be more green (as some people prefer), you can add cilantro or parsley. This is typically served 'wet', along with idli / thosai and sambar. As it sits, the coconut will absorb more liquid; it is also tasty in its drier (though still moist) form.

> 1 cup fresh / frozen grated coconut (if using desiccated, add 3 Tbsp. coconut milk)
> 1 onion, chopped
> 1 Tbsp. ginger, chopped
> 3 cloves garlic
> 1–3 green chilies
> about 10 curry leaves
> 1 tsp. salt
> 1 Tbsp. lime juice
> water as needed

1. Combine ingredients in food processor and pulse until well blended, about 5 minutes total. Add water as needed. Stop and scrape down sides as needed. Serve room temperature.

Green Tomato Chutney with Apples

(1 hr, makes a little under 1 qt.)

In America, this is the perfect end-of-season chutney, using up the tomatoes that didn't have a chance to ripen. It balances sweet, tangy, spicy, and salty, but the fabulous part of making your own chutney is that you can easily adjust seasonings to taste. So if you want it a bit sweeter, add a little more jaggery; if you want less heat, reduce the cayenne, or omit it entirely.

I've combined mine with apples and other fall flavors. For a more traditional version, substitute in more green tomatoes for the apples, and use white wine vinegar.

This chutney would be delicious at the Thanksgiving table. It's also terrific with rice and curry, of course!

2 Tbsp. vegetable oil
1 tsp. black mustard seed
1 onion, chopped (about 1 cup)
4 cups green tomatoes, chopped
2 green apples, chopped
1 oz. ginger, minced
1 cup apple cider vinegar
2 Tbsp. jaggery or brown sugar
¼–½ tsp. cayenne
1 tsp. fennel seeds
3 whole cloves
1 stick cinnamon
½–1 tsp. salt, optional

1. Sauté onions in oil with black mustard seed in a saucepan on medium-high high until onions are golden-translucent, stirring regularly.

2. Add remaining ingredients, bring to a boil, turn down to a simmer, cover, and cook 45 minutes, stirring occasionally.

Variation: Add ½ cup sultanas or chopped apricots for a fruitier version.

Note: Will keep refrigerated for a week or two in the fridge; follow proper canning instructions to store safely for months in the pantry; refrigerate after opening.

Mango-Ginger Chutney

(45 minutes, serves 8)

You don't actually need to cook a chutney—you can just chop up some fruit and mix it with spices and serve; that would be common in Sri Lanka. But I prefer a more blended chutney, with a mellower flavor. A great quick appetizer for a party is serving this with crackers and vegan cheese.

- 3 fresh mangoes, peeled and chopped (a ripe, 12 oz. mango will produce about 1 cup of fruit)
- 1 rounded tsp. salt
- 1 cup malt vinegar
- 3 dried chilies (optional)
- 3 Tbsp. fresh ginger, peeled and chopped fine
- ¾–1 cup sugar
- ⅓ cup sultanas (golden raisins)
- 1 rounded tsp. Sri Lankan curry powder

1. Put mango pieces in a large bowl and sprinkle with salt.

2. Remove stalks and seeds from chilies (if used) and soak chilies in a little vinegar for 10 minutes. Combine vinegar, ginger, and chilies in a blender and blend (you can alternatively pound the chilies with a mortar and pestle and grate the ginger in).

3. Put blended mixture in a stainless steel pan with curry powder and sugar and bring to a boil. Simmer, uncovered, for 15 minutes.

4. Add mangoes and sultanas. Turn heat back to medium-high and cook, stirring occasionally, until thick and syrupy.

5. Cool and serve with rice and curries, or add to a sandwich—it's great with vegan cheese or chickpea curry. You can also use the slightly more liquid version as a salad dressing.

Note: You can substitute green apples, pears, apricots, etc. for mangoes. Or mix and match!

Note 2: If not eating immediately, store in a jar in the fridge for a few weeks, or in the pantry for months, if canned and sterilized properly.

Bitter Gourd Sambol / Paavakkai Sambol

(15 minutes + 1 hour draining time, serves 8)

Bitter gourd is quite bitter! Seasoning it with turmeric and salt will draw the bitterest water to the surface to be blotted off, and deep-frying also tempers the bitterness. But still, a hint remains, adding an unusual flavor to this accompaniment.

- 1 bitter gourd, sliced thin (about 2 cups)
- 1 tsp. ground turmeric
- 1 tsp. salt
- 1 dozen curry leaves
- ¼ red onion, sliced
- 6 cherry tomatoes, sliced
- 3 green chilies, chopped
- oil for deep frying

1. Mix bitter gourd with turmeric and salt and let sit for an hour. Drain and blot dry with paper towels.

2. Heat oil and deep fry first the curry leaves, and then the bitter gourd in batches, removing to plates lined with paper towels.

3. Mix fried bitter gourd with tomatoes, chilies, and curry leaves and serve with rice and curries.

Chili Onion Sambol / Lunu Miris Sambol

(10 minutes, serves 8)

This classic Sri Lankan sambol is a simple way to add heat and tang to any meal. Sambols are particularly nice for pepping up leftovers, or helping to add spicy elements to the table for those who enjoy them, while leaving main dishes mild for those who prefer them that way.

>   1 onion, chopped coarsely
>   3 dried red chilies
>   1–2 tsp. cayenne
>   1–2 tsp. lime juice
>   1 tsp. salt

1. Combine ingredients in a food processor (alternatively, mince onion fine and then combine ingredients with mortar and pestle). Serve with hoppers, thosai, or whatever you like. Great on sandwiches too!

Coconut Sambol / Thengai-Poo, or Pol Sambol

(10 minutes, serves 8)

This is meant to be an accompaniment—make a batch (it keeps for weeks in the fridge) and then put a teaspoon or two on your plate with your rice / bread and curries. In Sri Lanka, they would just use straight up cayenne, instead of a mix of cayenne and paprika, which would make it fiercely spicy. If I were only going to make one accompaniment for the rest of my life, pol sambol would be my choice, although seeni sambol would be a very close second.

> 1 cup desiccated unsweetened coconut
> 3 Tbsp. hot coconut milk (I heat mine in the microwave)
> 1 rounded tsp. salt
> 1 rounded tsp. cayenne
> 2 rounded tsp. paprika
> 2–3 Tbsp. lime juice, to taste
> 1 medium onion, minced fine

1. Reconstitute coconut in a large bowl with the hot milk. I recommend using your fingers to squeeze the milk through the coconut. (If you can get fresh or frozen grated coconut, that is, of course, even better, and you can skip this step.)

2. Add salt, cayenne, paprika, lime juice, and onion. Mix thoroughly with your hand, rubbing ingredients together until well blended.

Note: If you don't feel that your onion is minced sufficiently fine (ideally, to match the texture of the coconut), you can use a food processor to chop it more finely, or grind it with a mortar and pestle. You can grind just the onions, or the whole mixture.

Eggplant Sambol / Kaththarikkai Sambol

(1 hour prep, 20 minutes cooking, serves 8)

My vegetarian friends are particularly fond of this dish. It offers a bright note, with its raw onion and lime juice, that wakes up a plate of rice and curry..

- 1 eggplant
- 1 rounded tsp. salt
- 1 rounded tsp. ground turmeric
- oil for deep frying
- 3 fresh green chilies, sliced thin
- 1 medium onion, sliced thin
- lime juice
- ¼ cup coconut milk, optional

1. Cut eggplant into quarters lengthwise and then slice thinly. Rub with salt and turmeric, spread on a few layers of paper towels and leave at least 1 hour. Bitter water will rise to the surface of the eggplant; blot that water with more paper towels. This will make for much tastier eggplant.

2. Heat about an inch of oil in a deep frying pan and fry eggplant slices slowly until brown on both sides. Lift out with Chinese spider (mesh metal spoon) and put in a dry bowl.

3. Mix with remaining ingredients; serve warm.

Ginger Sambol / Injii Sambol

(10 minutes, serves 4)

This was a new recipe to me, discovered in the process of researching this cookbook, and I was surprised to find how much I loved it; it's become a staple at my table. Both Kevin and I love ginger (which is also supposedly quite good for you).

> ¼ cup minced fresh ginger
> 1 cup fresh grated coconut
> 1–3 green chilies, seeded and chopped
> 1 cup chopped red onion
> 1 sprig mint leaves
> 1 Tbsp. lime juice
> ½ tsp. salt
> pinch of jaggery or dark brown sugar

1. Combine ingredients in food processor, blender, or mortar-and-pestle and process until well-blended. Serve, garnished with fresh mint.

NOTE: May be frozen for later use.

Kale Sambol

(20 minutes, serves 8)

I had never been a big kale fan, but my friend Roshani completely converted me with her Aunty Indranee's use of kale in this traditional sambol. In Sri Lanka, this would have been made with a native green, gotu kola, but kale is an excellent substitute (you can also try any other leafy greens, like beet greens, mustard greens, or rainbow chard).

For this preparation, kale is chopped small and tenderized with lime juice. When mixed with the coconut, tomatoes, sugar, and salt, the result is a tasty and addictive sambol that has become an essential component to many of our meals.

Note: This can be served immediately, but best if allowed to sit and blend for an hour or so. It will keep in the fridge for a good week—refresh with a little extra lime juice as needed.

> 1 bunch kale, leaves stripped off (stems discarded)
> 1 medium onion, minced
> 1 cup shredded unsweetened coconut
> 1–2 cups cherry tomatoes, chopped
> juice of 2 small limes (about 2–3 Tbsp.)
> 1–2 Tbsp. sugar
> 1 tsp. fine salt

1. Pulse kale in food processor until completely shredded into small bits.

2. Add onion, coconut, tomato, lime juice, sugar, salt. Mix thoroughly.

Plantain Sambol

(20 minutes, serves 4 as accompaniment)

Plantains are staple foods throughout Sri Lanka and the region, the main fare of millions of people for centuries. They're rich sources of complex carbohydrates, vitamins, and minerals, and are easily digestible. This traditional Jaffna-style plantain sambol offers a luscious, spicy-tangy bite, and is a great way to perk up a plate of rice and curry.

> 2 large ripe plantains (about 3 cups)
> ½ tsp. salt
> ½ tsp. turmeric powder
> oil for frying
> 6–8 dry red chilies
> 2 Tbsp. vinegar
> 1 tsp. black or brown mustard seeds
> 1 ½ tsp. sugar
> 1–2 minced shallots (about ½ cup)
> 1 chopped green fingerhot chili
> ½ tsp. salt, optional

1. Peel plantains and dice, then toss with ½ tsp. salt and turmeric.

2. Heat oil and fry diced plantain until golden; remove to a plate lined with kitchen towels and set aside.

3. Combine dry chilies, vinegar, mustard seeds and sugar to a smooth paste (in a blender or using a mortar-and-pestle).

4. Combine chili paste with shallots, chilies, and fried plantains. Taste and add ½ tsp. salt if desired. Serve as an accompaniment to rice and curries.

Rose Sambol

(10 minutes, serves 8)

When you have an overabundance of roses, you might make rose sambol. Is it the prettiest sambol? I think it might be. Be sure to use organic rose petals that haven't been treated with pesticides or herbicides.

- 20 roses, stalks removed, petals rinsed
- 1 cup red onion, sliced
- 1 cup fresh grated coconut
- 5 dried red chilies, broken into pieces
- 2 Tbsp. lime juice
- 1 tsp. salt

1. In a mortar and pestle or food processor, combine ingredients until well blended. Taste and adjust seasonings. Serve with rice and curry, roti, or anywhere else you'd use sambol.

Sweet Onion Sambol / Seeni Sambol

(1 hour, serves 8)

The Sri Lankan version of caramelized onions is sweet, spicy, and tangy. It's important to cook the onions slowly—all the liquid in the onion must evaporate if you want the sambol to keep well. Made properly, this dish can keep for several weeks in the fridge, so you can enjoy a little with each curry meal for quite a long time. An essential accompaniment for hoppers, and delicious with many other meals.

> ½ cup vegetable oil
> 4 medium onions, finely sliced
> 2 rounded tsp. cayenne
> 1 1-inch cinnamon stick
> 3 cloves
> 3 cardamom pods
> 1 stalk curry leaves
> 1 tsp. salt, or to taste
> 2 Tbsp. tamarind pulp
> 2 Tbsp. sugar

1. Heat oil in a large frying pan and start sautéing onions on medium-low. Add cinnamon, cloves, cardamom, curry leaves, and chill powder; continue cooking, stirring occasionally, until soft and transparent, about 30 minutes.

2. After about 30 minutes, cover pan, and simmer 10 minutes.

3. Uncover pan and continue simmering, stirring occasionally, until liquid evaporates and oil starts to separate from other ingredients. Season to taste with salt.

4. Remove from heat, stir in sugar and tamarind pulp, and allow to cool before putting in a clean dry jar. Use in small quantities.

Eggplant Pickle / Brinjal Moju

(20 minutes prep + 30 min. cooking time, feeds 8 as an accompaniment)

Eggplant was the one thing I wouldn't eat as a kid—I had a visceral reaction to the texture. But I adore it now, due to preparations like this, which really transform the texture—the eggplant here is a little chewy, a little soft, and supremely flavorful. If you leave the onions whole, they'll retain a little crunch when you bite into them; it's also fine to cut them and let them soften and crisp up more.

We call it a pickle, but brinjal moju is a quick-pickle—you can eat it right away, though it's even tastier after the flavors (sweet, spicy, tangy) have had a chance to meld for a few hours. It's terrific on a sandwich too! Try brinjal moju with coconut roti and big slices of grilled portobello mushroom (oil and salt and grill for a few minutes) for a hearty and delicious vegan lunch.

(Thanks to Samanthi Hewakapuge for tips on how her family prepares this!)

NOTE: Pearl onions can be a little tricky to find in America; I often buy mine frozen at the Indian grocery store. They thaw well for use in preparations like this. But shallots also work; you want that type of delicate flavor.

1 lb. eggplant (any kind), cut into thick matchstick shapes (about 2 inches long)
½ tsp. turmeric
1 tsp. salt
oil for deep frying

- 1 ½ cup shallots or pearl onions (cut large ones down to about 1 in.)
- 3–4 green finger hot chilies (or 10–15 Thai chilies)
- 1 Tbsp. ginger, peeled and chopped
- 3 cloves garlic, peeled and chopped
- 1–3 tsp. cayenne (depending on how hot you want it)
- 1 Tbsp. ground mustard
- 1 ½–2 Tbsp. sugar
- ⅓ cup vinegar

1. Place eggplant in a bowl, add turmeric, salt, and enough water to cover. Leave for at least 10 minutes; if you need to leave it to sit for longer, that's fine.

2. Take the eggplant out by handfuls and squeeze the water out, transferring to another bowl or plate.

3. Heat oil in a deep pan and fry eggplant in batches (to golden-brown), removing to a plate lined with paper towels.

4. Use the same oil to fry the shallots or pearl onions, then fry the green chilies, removing to the paper towel-lined plate.

5. Pound ginger and garlic together in a mortar and pestle (or combine in food processor).

6. In a large bowl, combine ginger-garlic paste with remaining ingredients, stirring to dissolve the sugar. Taste and adjust flavors.

7. Stir in shallots and green chilies, then gently stir-in the eggplant. Set aside for a few hours to let the flavors blend, then serve with rice and curry, or with bread.

NOTE: Brinjal moju will keep in the fridge for a few weeks, or follow proper canning procedures to store for longer. Makes a little over a pint for canning—eggplant cooks down quite a lot.

Lime Pickle

(15 minutes + a few weeks of preserving time, makes about 1 quart jar)

Tart, spicy, and salty, with a hint of aromatic spices, lime pickle is a wonderful complement to your meal. I first encountered a simple version of preserved limes in Little Women, where the schoolgirls had been banned from eating them. I had to learn more about why pickled limes might be banned:

"...they were sold from glass jars on top of candy-store counters, and some families even bought them by the barrel. Because the import tariff for pickled limes was quite low – importers fought to keep them classed as neither fresh fruit nor pickle – children could buy them cheaply, often for a penny apiece. Kids chewed, sucked, and traded pickled limes at school (and not just at recess) for decades, making the limes the perennial bane of New England schoolteachers. Doctors tended to disapprove of the limes...in 1869 a Boston physician wrote that pickled limes were among the "unnatural and abominable" substances consumed by children with nutritional deficiencies." Parents, however, seemed generally content for children to indulge themselves in the pickled-lime habit."—*Pickling*, Linda Ziedrich

Since pickled limes are quite salty, be sure to pair them with curries that are less so, for a beautifully balanced meal.

> 8 limes
> ¼ cup kosher salt
> ¼ cup vegetable oil
> 1 tsp. black mustard seed

1 tsp. fennel seed
1 tsp. fenugreek seed
2 stalks curry leaves (about two dozen leaves)
1 tsp. cayenne (optional)
1 tsp. turmeric
¼ cup lime juice (plus more as needed)

1. Quarter limes. Rub salt into limes, then transfer limes to sterilised glass jars. Seal and let sit for three days; once a day, open the jars and press the limes down, squeezing juice out. At the end of three days, the rinds should have yellowed, and the limes should be submerged in juice; if not fully submerged, add more lime juice to cover.

   NOTE: At this point, you have preserved limes, and you can eat them as is. If you let them sit for a few more weeks, the flavors will mellow and blend harmoniously. Many cuisines use preserved limes; it's common in that case to remove the flesh of the lime (which will be very salty), and only retain the rind / pith, which may be sliced and used in various dishes. Or, continue on with your entire limes to make lime pickle.

2. In a sauté pan, heat oil on high, add mustard seeds, and cook until they start to pop.

3. Turn down heat to medium and add remaining spices (if you'd prefer a smoother result, you may roughly grind spices before adding), preserved limes, and lime juice. Cook 10–15 minutes, stirring occasionally. (If you'd prefer a brighter, more fresh-fruit flavor, you may omit cooking the limes here, and simply pour the tempered spice mix over the limes in a bowl, combining well.)

4. Turn seasoned limes into sterilised glass jars, pressing down to compress. Set aside for 2 weeks to develop flavors; once a day, invert the jars so the seasoned liquid may permeate all the limes. Serve as an accompaniment to rice and curries.

NOTE: Once opened, store in the fridge for up to six months, or follow proper canning procedures for long-term pantry storage. When storing, a layer of oil on top of the limes will aid in preservation.

Mango Pickle / Maankai Oorukkai

(20 minutes, serves 8)

This is a fiery, fruity accompaniment that will keep refrigerated for a long time—you can add a little to your plate of rice and curry whenever you want to kick things up a bit. It's also tasty with vegan cheese and crackers, or layered in a sandwich.

- 2 cups raw mango (about 2 large), cubed small
- 3 Tbsp. oil
- 6–8 curry leaves
- 1 Tbsp. black mustard seed
- 1 Tbsp. ginger, chopped fine
- 1 Tbsp. garlic, chopped fine
- 3 green chilies, chopped
- 3 Tbsp. cayenne
- 1 tsp. ground turmeric
- ¼ cup vinegar
- 1 cup water
- 1 tsp. salt

1. Heat oil in a large frying pan and sauté mustard seeds, curry leaves, ginger, garlic, and chili on medium-high for a few minutes, stirring, until they start to smell cooked instead of raw.

2. Add cayenne, turmeric, vinegar, water, and salt; cook down to a thick pickling paste, about five minutes. Turn off heat and allow to cool for fifteen minutes or so.

3. Add mango to pan and mix well to combine. Store in the fridge and eat within a year or so, or fill canning jars and seal properly for seriously long-term storage). Serve with congee or other mild dishes.

Quick-Pickled Cucumber-Carrot Relish

(10 minutes + 10 minutes pickling time, serves 8)

This relish grew out of a need to use the last of my pickling cucumbers from the garden (we'd already pickled so many!), and a recipe from Jehan at Island Smile (https://www.islandsmile.org).

Their original recipe was a simple quick pickle, and you could certainly do just that, for a fresh note on your rice and curry plate or in your sandwich; it reminds me of the quick pickles you find in Japanese and Vietnamese cuisine, retaining a little toothsome bite.

If you'd like, though, you can add an extra step, tempering some mustard and fennel seeds to add a seasoned complex note to the dish. Tempering spices in hot oil is a classic South Asian technique, and I really love what it does for these pickled veggies.

- 2 Tbsp. vegetable oil, optional
- 1 tsp. black or brown mustard seeds, optional
- 1 tsp. fennel seeds, optional
- 3 Tbsp. sugar
- ½ c white vinegar
- 1 Tbsp. red chili flakes
- 2 tsp. salt
- 3 cucumbers, sliced in paper-thin rounds
- 3 carrots, sliced in paper-thin rounds
- 3 green chilies chopped fine
- 1 medium onion (red or yellow), sliced fine

1. OPTIONAL: Heat oil in a small frying pan, add mustard seeds, cook until seeds begin to pop, releasing mustard scent. Turn off heat and stir in fennel seeds, frying for another 30 seconds or so. Let cool.

2. In a large bowl, combine sugar, vinegar, chili, and salt.

3. Add chopped veggies and mix (easiest to do with your clean hands.

4. If using tempered spice oil, pour into bowl and mix well.

5. Let sit 10 minutes or so, then enjoy!

NOTE: Will keep for about a week in the refrigerator.

Spicy Pineapple Pickle / Achar

(10 minutes, makes about 4 cups)

In the dead of a Chicago winter, when the snow is piled high outside the door, and it feels like you'll never be warm again, a sweet-spicy-tangy pineapple pickle will liven up your plate of rice and curry, and remind you that sunny lands do exist.

- 2 cups pineapple, cut into bite-size pieces
- 1 shallot, peeled, cut in half, and sliced thin
- 1 cup apple tfrg vinegar
- 1 Tbsp. sugar
- 1 tsp. fine salt
- 2 tsp. black peppercorns
- 2 tsp. cayenne

1. Combine ingredients in a small pot, bring to a boil, simmer 5 minutes.

2. Let cool. Can be eaten right away, but better after it's had a day or two to meld flavors.

NOTE 1: Store in the fridge and use within a few weeks; for longer pantry storage, follow safe canning procedures.

NOTE 2: If you want it a little less pungent/spicy, you can dilute by adding ½–1 cup water to the vinegar, and/or reduce the peppercorns / cayenne.

Cucumber-Tomato Raita

(10 minutes, serves 8)

I'm afraid I've never picked up the habit myself of eating yogurt with curry, but many of my friends swear by raita, and the ones who have trouble with the spiciness of some of the dishes really appreciate the cooling properties of yogurt. I often make some raita to accompany a spicy meal when serving guests.

- 1 medium cucumber
- 2–4 plum tomatoes, chopped coarsely
- 2 fresh green chilies, seeded and chopped (optional)
- ½ tsp. salt
- freshly ground black pepper to taste
- 1 cup vegan yogurt

1. Grate cucumber coarsely; squeeze out excess water.

2. Mix all ingredients well; serve cold.

Leeks Fried with Chili

(50 minutes, serves 8)

his accompaniment offers a little extra heat and onion-y zing to a plate of rice and curry.

>   4 medium leeks
>   ¼ cup oil
>   ½ rounded tsp. ground turmeric
>   1 ½ rounded tsp. cayenne
>   1 rounded tsp. salt

1. Rinse dirt off outside of leeks. Discard any tough or withered leaves, but do use the green portions as well as the white.

2. With a sharp knife, slice the leeks thinly across the stalk, making thin rings / chiffonade; when you're slicing the green leaves, make a tight bundle in your hands for easier slicing.

3. Wash the sliced leeks very thoroughly. The soil trapped between the leaves won't actually taste particularly bad, but the grittiness is unpleasant. I recommend not simply running the sliced leeks under a colander—rather, put them in a large bowl of water and wash them vigorously, changing the water at least three times. This is labor-intensive, but well worth it.

4. Heat oil in a large saucepan and add the leeks. Sauté, stirring for 5 minutes, then add the remaining ingredients and stir until well blended.

5. Cover and cook over low heat for 30 minutes, stirring occasionally. The leeks will reduce in volume. Uncover and cook, stirring, until liquid evaporates and leeks appear slightly oily. Serve hot.

Spiced Tomato Jam / Thakkaali Yaam

(1 hour, makes 2 cups jam)

This traditional Sri Lankan condiment, featuring rich tomato flavor gently spiced and sweetened with jaggery, is typically served with thosai, pittu, idli, or rice. It's also delicious as a component in appetizers, spread on breakfast toast, as a topping for grilled vegetables—the possibilities are endless.

> 1 lb. tomatoes, diced (about 1 ½ cups)
> 3 cloves
> 2 cardamom pods
> 1 star anise
> 1 tsp. peppercorns
> zest of 1 lemon
> juice of 1 lemon (about 3 Tbsp.)
> 1 cup jaggery or dark brown sugar
> 1 tsp. salt

1. In a hot dry pan, toast spices until aromatic. Let cool and grind to powder.

2. Add diced tomatoes to a medium saucepan with remaining ingredients, and bring to a boil. Stir until sugar has dissolved, then turn heat to low and cover.

3. Simmer about 40 minutes. Remove lid, and if mixture is still liquid, simmer uncovered a little longer, until it thickens to jam texture. Use wherever you'd use jam or chutney.

Variation: Replace half of the tomatoes with chopped pineapple.

Note: Jars can be stored in refrigerator for up to 2 weeks.

SOUPS

Coconut Milk Gravy / Sothi

Coriander Soup / Kothamalli Rasam

Curried Pumpkin Soup

Herbal Porridge / Kola Kenda

Coconut Milk Gravy / Sothi

(45 minutes + soaking time, serves 8)

This is a delicious traditional accompaniment for stringhoppers, served with a little coconut sambol. When I last visited Sri Lanka, that was one of my favorite meals to have for breakfast, in the very early morning at the hotel, while I was still jet-lagged. It's quite soothing. This makes a fairly large quantity, suitable for feeding several people; just cut ingredients in half for a smaller portion.

- 1–4 Tbsp. fenugreek seeds, soaked for two hours beforehand
- 1 Tbsp. toasted rice powder (optional)
- 1 large onion, diced
- 12 curry leaves
- 1 2-inch cinnamon stick
- 2 fresh green chilies, seeded and chopped
- ½ tsp. ground turmeric
- 1 tsp. salt
- 2 cups water
- 1 russet potato, peeled and cubed (optional)
- 3 cups coconut milk
- 1–2 Tbsp. lime juice, to taste

Note 1: Traditionally, this dish was made with quite a lot of fenugreek; modern recipes tend to reduce to about 1 tablespoon, instead of 4. But fenugreek is a potent galactagogue, so if you're making this dish for a nursing mother, you may want to go old-school.

Note 2: Toasted rice powder is used throughout Asia (especially in Thai cooking) to thicken and add flavor and fragrance to dishes. It's best made fresh, in the quantities needed. To make, take 1 tablespoon rice and sauté over medium heat in a dry pan for 10–15 minutes, stirring constantly. It'll release a beautifully nutty, toasted scent. Then grind to a powder—I use a coffee grinder that I keep dedicated for spices, but you could also use a food processor, or the traditional mortar and pestle.

1. Put all the ingredients except the last two (coconut milk, and lime juice) in a saucepan. Bring to a boil, then turn down heat and simmer, covered, until onions are reduced to a pulp and the potatoes are cooked, about 30 minutes.

2. Stir well, add thick coconut milk and heat without bringing dish to a boil. Stir in lime juice, and/or additional salt to taste. Simmer a minute or two longer, stirring, and then serve hot, with stringhoppers or rice.

Coriander Soup / Kothamalli Rasam

(20 minutes, serves 8)

I don't make this often myself, but it's one of my mother's favorite dishes. For a very simple meal, serve it to sip with plain rice, with perhaps a little sambol. It's lovely when you're feeling a little under the weather; the tang and slight spiciness are just the thing to settle you.

> 1 Tbsp. tamarind paste
> 1 cup hot water
> 2 cloves garlic, sliced
> ¾ rounded tsp. fresh ground black pepper
> 1 rounded tsp. ground cumin
> 4 cups cold water
> 2 rounded tsp. salt
> 2 Tbsp. chopped fresh coriander / cilantro leaf
> 2 tsp. vegetable oil
> 2 Tbsp. coriander seeds
> 1 rounded tsp. black mustard seeds
> 8 curry leaves

1. Dissolve tamarind paste in hot water.

2. Put tamarind liquid, garlic, pepper, cumin, water, salt, and coriander leaves into a saucepan and bring it to a boil.

3. Turn heat down and simmer for 10 minutes.

4. In another pan, heat the oil and sauté the coriander seeds, mustard seeds, and curry leaves until leaves are toasted. Add to the simmering liquid and serve hot.

Curried Pumpkin Soup

with Sri Lankan Roasted Pumpkin Seeds

(1 hour, serves 8)

I live in Oak Park, just outside Chicago, so autumn is definitely gourd season—pumpkins everywhere. When my children were little, we took them to pumpkin patches; now we try to grow pumpkins in our garden, with mixed success, and carve messy jack-o-lanterns, making sure to save the seeds for roasting. So it just seems right to enjoy a curried pumpkin soup on a bright October day, when the sun is glowing through the turning leaves, gold and crimson.

> 1 batch pumpkin curry
> 32 oz. vegetable stock
> 1 cinnamon stick
> 2 Tbsp. lime juice
> ½–1 tsp. additional salt, to taste
> Optional garnishes: coconut milk, marigold petals, Sri Lankan-style roasted pumpkin seeds

1. Make pumpkin curry in a large pot. (I recommend peeling the pumpkin if you plan to use it for soup.)

2. Add stock and cinnamon stick, bring to a boil, turn down and simmer for 20 minutes or so, stirring occasionally.

3. Remove cinnamon stick and purée until smooth. Optional, but makes it pretty and gives the soup a velvety texture—an immersion blender makes this job much easier than trying to transfer hot soup into a blender safely.

4. Stir in lime juice, taste, add salt if needed.

5. Serve hot, garnished with a swirl of thick coconut milk, edible marigold petals, and roasted pumpkin seeds.

ROASTED PUMPKIN SEEDS, SRI LANKAN-STYLE

The white seeds you get from a carving pumpkin are actually pumpkin seed husks—if you really wanted to, you could do a lot of work trying to get to the green seeds (known as pepitas) inside. Pepitas are delicious, but are actually usually harvested from pumpkins that don't produce these white husks. But don't throw these away—big white pumpkin 'seeds' are great roasted too, adding in some extra fiber and a nice crunch.

You could just toss them with a little oil and salt, but why not kick it up a notch? Try them Sri Lankan-style—these are a terrific topping for a curried pumpkin soup. Salty + sweet + savory + spicy. Perfect.

> 1 cup white pumpkin seeds, rinsed and dried
> 2 Tbsp. vegetable oil
> 1 tsp. salt
> 1 tsp. brown sugar
> 1 tsp. Sri Lankan roasted curry powder (with or without ½ tsp. cayenne, your choice)

1. Preheat oven to 300°F.

2. Toss seeds with oil and spices.

3. Spread in a flat layer on a sheet of foil and roast for about 40 minutes, until dry and crispy. (Keep an eye on them for the last 5–10 minutes of roasting, to make sure they don't burn.)

4. Enjoy as a snack on their own, or topping your favorite autumn dishes.

Herbal Porridge / Kola Kenda

(5–10 minutes, plus time to cook rice, serves 4)

This herbal leaf porridge is considered tremendously healthful, and is often drunk straight up first thing in the morning in Sri Lanka, or mixed with rice for a light breakfast. It's typically lightly seasoned—the fresh herbs carry the flavor, with just a little salt and a touch of black pepper. But you can amend it as desired—fresh ginger is a common addition, and if you prefer a sweeter breakfast, you can always stir in a little jaggery.

Kola kenda is supposed to stave off all manner of digestive difficulties, but I'm enough of a gardener to find those claims unlikely, given that the choice of herbs is so variable. But a quick internet search will find far more detail on the subject, if you're so inclined. It's a staple of the Ayurvedic medicine tradition. Regardless of the health claims, it's a fresh and tasty start to your day.

You can buy powdered versions of the traditional herbs found in Sri Lanka online, the result looks rather unappealing and murky, compared to the brightness of fresh herbs. I use a combination of fresh curry leaves, cilantro, and fenugreek (from a frozen packet), but you can experiment with the dark leafy herbs of your choice. Straight-up cilantro works fine, for example.

Traditional herbs would include gotu kola (*Centella asiatica*), sessile joyweed (*Alternanthera sessilis*, known as mukunuwenna in Sri Lanka), haathawariya (*Asparagus racemosus*), welpenela [*Cardiospermum halicacabum (Sapindaceae)*], aubergine (Elabatu), or polpala (*Aerva lanata*).

1 bunch fresh herbs (about 1 ½ cups)
1 cup coconut milk
2 cups water
1 tsp. salt
½ tsp. pepper (optional)
1 cup cooked rice (I use red samba rice)
2–3 Tbsp. jaggery (optional)

1. Combine herbs with coconut milk and water in blender and puree until smooth. (Traditionally, the herbs would have been mashed with a mortar and pestle.) Add salt, and pepper if using.

2. Stir herbal soup into rice in a pot, bring to a boil, then turn it down and simmer for a few minutes, stirring, until well blended. Serve hot, with jaggery if desired.

Come to me.
I will make you rice.

Thick, white, sticky rice,
clinging to your fingertips.
Dark, wild rice,
scented like fields in autumn.

Slender grains of basmati rice,
aromatic, rich with rose essence,
saffron-gold-threaded,
graced by sultanas,
by almonds and cashews...

Come to me, and I will feed you rice
made by my own small hands.

GRAINS

Biryani

Golden Rice Pilaf

Hoppers / Appam

Jaggery Pongal / Sakkarai Pongal

Kundu Thosai / Paniyaram

Milk Rice / Kiri Bath (with Bottle Gourd variation)

Millet Roti, with Coconut and Jaggery / Kurakkan Roti

Red Rice Congee

Roti, Plain / Kothambu Roti

Roti Stir-Fry, Chopped / Kottu Roti

Savory Rice Pancakes / Thosai

Spinach Pittu / Keerai Pittu

Steamed Rice Cakes / Idli

Steamed Rice Flour and Coconut / Arisi-Maa Pittu

Steamed Rice Flour and Coconut with Milk / Pal Pittu

Stir-Fried Semolina / Uppuma

Stringhoppers / Idiyappam

Stringhopper Biryani / Idiyappam Biryani

Tamarind Rice with Black Lentils

Biryani

(1 hour, serves 6–8)

Biryani, derived from the Persian word berya, which means fried or roasted, is a rice-based dish made with spices and vegetables. It is generally more strongly spiced than a pilaf (though closely related), and commonly layered as part of its preparation. Sri Lankan biryani is spicier than Indian, and generally served with curries and sambols.

This has a lot of ingredients and may look a bit intimidating, but it's actually quite straightforward—mostly, you're just adding everything to one big pot, step-by-step. It isn't usually everyday food, given that it does take a while to cook, but if you have a special occasion to celebrate, biryani is an impressive crowd-pleaser. It will come out a bit dry, so I would serve it with a curry, or something else that offers a gravy. Even a vegan yogurt raita would work!

Note: If you don't have an oven-safe dutch oven, you can start this in a regular large pot and transfer it to a baking dish for the final step.

- 2 cups basmati rice
- 2 lbs. eggplant, green jackfruit, squash, mushrooms (singly or in combination)
- 1 tsp. ground coriander
- 1 tsp. ground cumin
- 1 tsp. black pepper
- 1 tsp. Sri Lankan curry powder
- 1 tsp. salt
- 1 Tbsp. vinegar
- 4 Tbsp. oil

1 cup cashew nuts
1 cup sultanas (golden raisins)
3 sliced onions
8–12 curry leaves
6 cardamom pods
6 cloves
1 stick cinnamon, broken in 3–6 pieces
1 cup thick coconut milk

1. Cook rice via usual method and set aside.

2. Cut vegetables into cubes and season with coriander, cumin, black pepper, and curry powder, together with salt and vinegar and set aside.

3. Heat oil over medium heat and lightly fry the cashew nuts and sultanas, stirring, and set aside.

4. In the same pan, fry the onions, curry leaves, cardamom pods, and cloves until golden brown.

5. Add the vegetables to the pan and sauté, stirring occasionally, until the vegetables are cooked through and the liquid has cooked off, about 20 minutes.

6. Add the rice and stir gently; add coconut milk and cinnamon, mixing gently. Simmer over a low flame for about five minutes, until well blended.

7. Serve on a flat dish and decorate with fried sultanas and cashew nuts.

Golden Rice Pilaf

(20 minutes, serves 4–6)

Here's where I cheat. When I'm having a party, I'd often like to serve biryani, as my mother would—but making biryani properly is a fair bit of work, and sometimes I just don't have time. So I often make this instead.

2 cups uncooked basmati rice
4 cups water
¼–½ cup sultanas (golden raisins)
¼–½ cup cashews
1 Tbsp. coconut oil or vegan butter
¼ tsp. salt
1–2 drops rose essence
½ tsp. saffron (you can use turmeric for a similar color, but it won't taste right)

1. Combine all ingredients in a large pot and bring to a boil.

Note: This is truly low-effort cooking—a tastier approach would be to sauté the cashews and sultanas in the vegan butter (with maybe a little sliced onion) in a separate pan, and then stir those into the cooked rice at the end, saving some to garnish the top of the dish with some fresh chopped coriander leaves.

2. Cover and turn heat down to simmer until rice is cooked, approximately 15 minutes.

Hoppers / Appam

(30–45 minutes + overnight fermenting time, makes 12)

If I had to pick the perfect Sri Lankan meal, this would be it. There's nothing like breaking off a crisp piece of hopper and scooping up some curry and a bit of seeni sambol. Delectable.

These rice flour pancakes have a unique shape; fermented batter is swirled in a special small hemispherical pan, so you end up with a soft, spongy center, and lacey, crispy sides—that contrast is the true glory of the hopper. Typically you'd make two plain hoppers per person, and maybe a sweet hopper to finish up.

Note: You can buy instant hopper mix, available online, and just add water, which will work fine, and doesn't require overnight planning ahead. Many diasporic Sri Lankans I know use that option regularly.

If you don't have a hopper pan, you can make hoppers in a regular frying pan; you just won't get quite as much of the crispy sides. It's a little time-consuming to make hoppers, since each one must be individually steamed for a few minutes, but with practice, you can have four hopper pans going on a stove at once. I'd recommend starting with just one pan at a time, though! Serve with curry and seeni sambol.

> 2 cups South Asian rice flour (or a mix of rice and wheat flour)
> 1 tsp. sugar
> pinch of baking powder
> ½ tsp. salt
> 2 cups coconut milk
> extra coconut milk and jaggery for sweet hoppers

1. Mix first five ingredients thoroughly in a large bowl, cover, and set in a warm, turned-off oven to ferment overnight. (In a cold climate,

fermentation may not occur without a little help—I turn my oven on to 250°, and when it's reached temperature, turn it off and put the covered bowl in the oven to stay warm.)

2. Mix again, adding water if necessary to make a quite thin, pourable batter.

3. Heat pan (grease if not non-stick) on medium, and when it's hot, pour about ⅓ cup batter into the center. Pick up the pan immediately and swirl the batter around, coating the cooking surface. The sides of the hopper should end up with holes in them: thin, lacy, and crisp—if the batter is coating the pan more thickly, mix in some hot water to thin it down. Cover and let cook for 2–4 minutes—you'll know it's ready when the sides have started to brown and the center is thoroughly cooked. A silicone spatula will help get the hopper out of the pan.

4. For sweet hoppers, after swirling, add a tablespoon of coconut milk and a teaspoon of jaggery to the center of the pan, then cook as usual.

Jaggery Pongal / Sakkarai Pongal

(30–40 minutes, serves 8–10)

For this one-pot celebration dish, rice is mixed with a little toasted mung bean and cooked down until very soft, close to custard texture. Sweeten the rice with jaggery and coconut milk, season with fried cashews, raisins, cardamom and saffron, and you have a dish fit for the gods—which was, in fact, what jaggery pongal was intended for. It was traditionally made to offer the gods as part of the harvest celebration of Pongal (typically around mid-January), and on other similarly celebratory occasions.

In modern times, many will use a pressure cooker or Instant Pot to bring the rice quickly to the right texture, but I go a bit more old school here, which requires stirring on the stovetop.

2 cups rice (white or red, your choice)
4 cups water
1 cup coconut milk
¼ cup green grams / mung bean, toasted in a dry pan
1 cup jaggery
1 tsp. salt
2 Tbsp. vegetable oil or vegan butter
¼ cup cashew nuts, chopped
¼ cup raisins
¼ tsp. ground cardamom
pinch of saffron threads
optional garnish: whole cashew nuts and raisins fried in more vegetable oil or vegan butter

1. Soak the toasted green grams for 30 minutes, then add to a large saucepan, along with rice and water. Bring to a boil, then cover and simmer 15–20 minutes, until rice is mostly cooked through.

2. Stir in jaggery and coconut milk, then cover and continue to cook, stirring periodically to keep from sticking. If you need to add more water, do so.

3. Meanwhile, heat the oil or vegan butter in a saucepan over medium heat. Add cashews and raisings and fry until cashews are golden brown. Stir them into the cooked rice mixture.

4. Add cardamom and saffron and continue to cook, stirring periodically, until rice has broken down, and the entire dish has a somewhat creamy texture (similar in appearance to risotto).

5. Remove from heat and cool. You can simply spoon it in to bowls for serving, or for a fancier presentation, mold into portions by pressing into greased cups, then unmold and serve garnished with additional fried cashews and raisins. A little fried ripe plantain would also go nicely with this, or fresh ripe mango.

Kundu Thosai / Paniyaram

(30–45 minutes + soaking and fermenting time, makes 25–30)

Kundu thosai are round lentil and flour 'pancake balls,' similar to Dutch poffertjes, Danish aebelskiver, or Japanese takoyaki in approach, and they can be made in the same kind of pan. I wouldn't be surprised to learn that they came to Sri Lanka by way of Dutch colonizers, though you'd need to consult a food historian to be sure!

Poffertjes use a pan with smaller (and more) indentations than aebelskiver—depending on your pan, you may need to adjust cooking time appropriately for your kundu thosai; larger balls will take a few minutes longer to cook through.

They're typically made with leftover thosai batter, but you can certainly just make kundu thosai straight up. Remember to start at least a day and a half before you plan to eat them, as there's a soaking lentils 6–8 hr step and a fermenting batter 6–8 hr step. They can be made with rice flour (traditional), wheat flour (softer), or a combination of the two.

Savory versions are sometimes dressed up with a little onion and chili (raw or sautéed briefly), and sweet versions add in jaggery, cardamom and fresh coconut. Do note that the sweet versions are still using fermented batter, so the sour-sweet flavor combo may not be what you expect; I have to admit that my kids have not quite decided if they approve or not!

Savory kundu thosai served with a little coconut chutney is a pretty perfect breakfast for me, and the lentils give a great healthy boost to your day.

    1 cup urad dal / black gram / ulunththu, skinless and split
    1 cup flour, divided
    ½ tsp. baking soda
    ½ tsp. salt

water to make batter
vegetable oil
Savory variation: ½–1 cup chopped onions and 1–3 chopped green chilies
Sweet variation: ¼–½ cup jaggery or brown sugar, ½ tsp. ground cardamom, and ½ cup fresh coconut

1. Soak black gram for 6–8 hours or overnight (I would usually start this the afternoon before I planned to serve them, so starting Saturday afternoon for Sunday brunch). Grind finely using a grinder or food processor, to a thick paste—add a little water if needed for smooth grinding.

2. In a frying pan, toast ½ cup flour on high heat, stirring constantly, until light brown (5–10 minutes).

3. Mix toasted flour, remaining ½ cup flour, baking soda, salt. Add in ground dal and sufficient water to mix and create a batter. You're aiming for a pourable batter, a little thicker than pancake batter; stir in water ½ cup at a time until you get the consistency right.

4. Set aside batter in a warm place to ferment for 6–8 hours or overnight. (If you're in a cool climate, a good option is an oven that's been warmed up and then turned off.) The batter should rise and likely double in bulk, so be sure there's enough room in your bowl for that; you may want to put something under it to catch any spills.

NOTE: If you haven't made coconut chutney yet, pause and make that now, so that it's ready when the kundu thosai start coming hot out of the pan.

5. Stir batter (it will deflate). Heat molded pan on medium heat and add a little oil to each indentation. When oil is hot, add a spoonful of batter to each. Use a skewer, fork, or chopsticks to turn the kundu thosai to cook on the other side. (In Denmark, knitting needles are traditional!)

6. Remove from molds when cooked through, a few minutes each; serve warm with coconut chutney (recommended). You can also serve with other chutneys or with curry.

SAVORY VARIATION: Chop some onion, green chili, and curry leaves; sauté in oil for a few minutes if you like, or leave raw. Stir into batter.

SWEET VARIATION: Add some jaggery or brown sugar, ground cardamom, and fresh grated coconut to the batter. Note that they'll look darker as they come off the pan, due to the caramelizing sugar in the batter.

Milk Rice / Kiri Bath

(with Bottle Gourd (Labu) variation)

(25–40 minutes, serves 4)

Kiri bath (pronounced 'buth'), rice cooked with coconut milk, is an essential part of Sinhalese culinary tradition in Sri Lanka. It's a required element on New Year's Day (celebrated in April on a lunar cycle), and often eaten on the first day of each month. Kiri bath is generally served with lunu miris or other spicy sambols, although some prefer it sweet, with jaggery.

Sri Lanka has been a multi-ethnic society for over 2000 years, and when my parents' Sinhalese neighbors made kiri bath, they would always bring some over to share with their Tamil friends. I didn't grow up cooking it myself, but it was always a particular treat when my Sinhalese friends made it for me. I love kiri bath with pol sambol plus a nice curry, and a little paruppu (dal / lentils) never goes amiss. Maybe a bit of brinjal moju (pickle) too!

I ran across an interesting variation through a cooking video (by Chandeena and her mother at Village Life[1]), where you add bottle gourd to the dish—it lends a lovely delicacy to the finished kiri bath, and may also serve to lighten it up a bit, for those who love the richness of flavor, but are perhaps being careful about their portion sizes of luscious rice and coconut milk.

    2 cups short grain white (or red) rice
    3 cups water
    2 cups coconut milk

---
[1] https://youtu.be/8EYvQ3S9ayU

1 ½ tsp. salt
2 cups shredded bottle gourd (or cucumber), optional

1. Put rice, bottle gourd (if using), and water in a pan and bring to a boil; cover, reduce heat to medium, and cook 15 minutes. The rice should be mostly cooked at this point, but it's fine if it's a little firm still. (Red rice may want an extra 5 minutes.)

2. Add coconut milk and salt, stir well. Cover the pan again, turn heat to low, and cook for a further 10–15 minutes, until the milk is entirely absorbed. (Red rice may want an extra 5 minutes here too.)

3. Traditionally, you'd let it cool a little, turn it onto a flat plate, and smooth it (using a spatula or banana leaves) into a firm, flat round. Mark it off in squares or diamond shapes, and serve with your favorite sambols.

Millet Roti, with Coconut and Jaggery / Kurakkan Roti

(30 minutes, serves 4–6)

Ready to up your roti game? Try making it with millet flour (you can buy whole grain millet and quickly grind it to flour yourself in a blender), mixed with coconut and jaggery; the sweetness pairs beautifully with a spicy curry or earthy dal. Finger millet is traditional, but other common varieties of millet will also work well for this; I use proso millet, which is easily found at my local grocery.

NOTE: for a gluten-free version, you can make this entirely with millet flour (as was typical in ancient Sri Lanka), but it will be more brittle; white wheat flour adds softness.

> 1 cup millet flour
> ½ cup white flour
> ½ tsp. fine salt
> 1 cup grated coconut
> ½ cup jaggery (or brown sugar)
> hot water (as required, around ½–¾ cup)
> 1 cup vegetable oil (enough to submerge rotis)

1. Combine first five ingredients in a bowl.

2. Add hot water slowly, mixing to make smooth dough.

3. Turn onto a board, oil your hands, and knead about 10 minutes (the dough will likely be a little sticky). Divide into sixteen portions and form little balls with the dough.

4. Pour oil into a flat tray; submerge balls in oil. (It's a lot of oil, but if you make roti regularly, you can save it and re-use it time after time.)

5. Heat a frying pan (either nonstick, or plan to drizzle a little oil in the pan as needed to prevent sticking). Take a ball of dough, flatten into a circle, and roll out (or use the heel of your hand to flatten) until fairly thin—as thin as you can get it without tearing. This requires a gentle touch, as millet dough is more prone to tearing than wheat dough.

6. Cook each roti separately on high, turning over after about thirty seconds to cook the other side. They will brown slightly. Remove to a plate, covering them each time with a clean dishtowel, to keep warm. Serve either warm or at room temperature.

Red Rice Congee

(30 minutes, serves 2)

While many may associate 'congee' with a Chinese breakfast dish, the word 'congee' actually comes from the Tamil word 'kanji'; it refers to a rice-based porridge, eaten throughout Asia. This variation is a comforting way to start your morning—a traditional breakfast made either with fresh rice or leftover, and served with a little jaggery to sweeten it. It's also good for building up the strength of the convalescent. Red rice can be purchased online, and is similar to brown rice in nutritional content. It has a mildly nutty flavor; a healthy choice for breakfast! You can make this with white or brown rice too, of course.

Some people prefer a more soupy version; just add more water at the end. Traditionally, you would smash the rice down with a spoon as a final step, to give it more of a porridge consistency, but personally, I prefer the distinct grains. Another option is to grind about half the cooked rice in a food processor after step 1, but that does mean one more thing to wash!

Other traditional accompaniments include fruit, nuts, or fiery luna miris sambol. This is a dish that easily adapts to your personal taste.

1 cup red rice
1 ¾ cups water
pinch of salt
2 Tbsp. vegetable oil
1 large onion, sliced thin
1 Tbsp. ginger, sliced thin
3 cloves garlic, sliced thin
2 green chilies, chopped
1 stalk curry leaves
1 tsp. salt

1 cup coconut milk
1 cup water
2–3 Tbsp. jaggery

1. In a pot, combine rice, 1 ¾ cups water, and pinch of salt. Bring to a boil, cover, cook 20 minutes, then turn off the heat and let sit 5 more minutes.

2. In a large frying pan, sauté onion, ginger, garlic, chilies, curry leaves, and salt in oil, until onions are golden-brown.

3. Add rice to pan and mix well; add coconut milk and water and simmer a few minutes to desired thickness. Serve hot, with jaggery.

Roti, Plain / Kothambu Roti

(30 minutes, serves 4–6)

If you haven't made bread before, you might be startled by how quick and easy it is! Fresh roti are a lovely treat, elevating a simple meal into something special.

> 1 cup all-purpose flour
> 1 ½ tsp. baking powder
> ¼ tsp. fine salt
> water (as required, around ½ cup)
> 1 cup vegetable oil (enough to submerge rotis)

1. Combine flour, baking powder, and salt in a bowl.

2. Add water slowly, then knead to make smooth dough, about 10 minutes (the dough should not be sticky). Divide into twelve portions and form little balls with the dough.

3. Pour oil into a flat tray; submerge balls in oil. (It's a lot of oil, but if you make roti regularly, you can save it and re-use it time after time.)

4. Heat a frying pan (either nonstick, or plan to drizzle a little oil in the pan as needed to prevent sticking). Take a ball of dough, flatten into a circle, and roll out until paper-thin—as thin as you can get it without tearing.

5. Cook each roti separately on high, turning over after about thirty seconds to cook the other side. They will brown slightly. Remove to a dishtowel, covering them each time, to keep warm. Serve either warm or at room temperature.

Roti Stir-Fry, Chopped / Kottu Roti

(30 minutes, serves 4)

This is one of my favorite Sri Lankan dishes, though I don't make it with as much flair as the street vendors, who wield massive knives chopping at furious speed. The curry sauce blends perfectly with the roti and the fresh vegetables, creating a soft, tender concoction.

- 4 rotis (or parathas or similar flatbreads), chopped coarsely
- 2–3 Tbsp. vegetable oil
- 1 red onion, chopped
- 3 green chilies, chopped
- 1 stalk curry leaves
- 1 cup green beans, chopped small
- 1 carrot, grated coarsely
- 1 leek, white and light green portion, sliced finely, grit washed off
- 1 cup leftover curry (any vegan curry will work, but it needs to have at least ½ cup of actual sauce)

1. Sauté onion, green chilies, and curry leaves in oil until lightly browned, about five minutes.

2. Add green beans, carrot, and leeks, and sauté until cooked through, about five more minutes.

3. Add rotis and mix thoroughly.

4. Add curry and mix thoroughly. Serve hot!

Note 1: As a variation, you can add half a chopped cabbage at step three, and reduce the amount of roti, for a more vegetal approach.

Note 2: I've made this with tortillas in a pinch, but rotis do a better job of sopping up the sauce. Naan is a little thick, so is not ideal, but if you're desperate and have nothing else on hand, needs must.

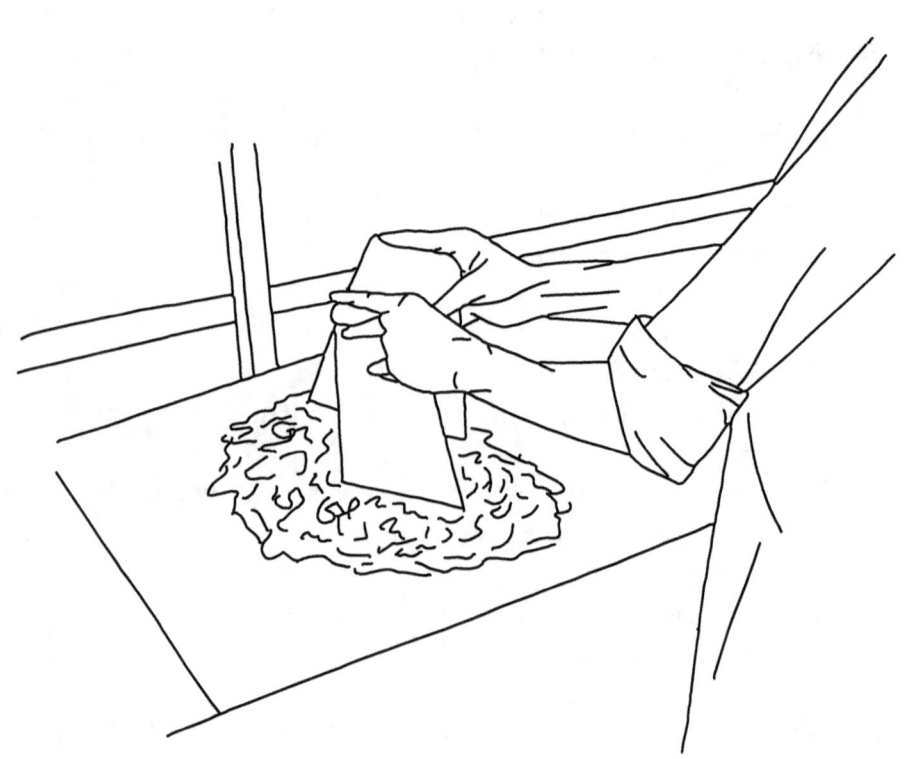

Savory Rice Pancakes / Thosai

(20 minutes + soaking, grinding, and fermenting time, serves 4)

Known as dosa in India, these tangy rice and lentil pancakes are delicious for breakfast or a light dinner, served with sambar and coconut chutney. For a more substantial version (masala thosai), add a spiced potato-onion filling.

You can make thosai from a just-add-water-and-oil mix, but making it from scratch is supposedly healthier, since it involves fermenting with wild bacteria.

> ½ cup idli or parboiled rice, washed
> ½ cup basmati rice, washed
> 1 cup split urad dal, washed
> 1 tsp. fenugreek seeds
> 1 tsp. salt

1. Mix rice, cover with water in a bowl. In a separate bowl, combine urad dal and fenugreek seeds, cover with water. Let soak for at least 4 hours.

2. Drain rice and grind in a food processor until very fine and smooth; add water if necessary. You're aiming for a thin pourable batter. Repeat with urad dal and fenugreek seeds.

3. Mix batters together in a large bowl with salt, cover, and set aside in a warm oven (turned off) overnight (or for at least 8 hours).

Note: If making masala thosai, make masala potatoes before cooking thosai; see below.

4. To make thosai, stir well, adding water if necessary to make a pourable batter.

5. Grease and heat a large frying pan on high; spoon about a half cup of batter (a ladle works well for this) onto the pan; spread it out with the back of the ladle to make a large circle.

6. Don't flip! When the bottom turns golden and crisp, and the top has thoroughly bubbled, use a spatula to remove from pan.

7. If making masala thosai, add a few spoons of potato mixture (below) to the center of the thosai; fold and serve hot, with chutney and sambar, or a vegetable curry.

Masala Potato Filling
    1 lb. russet potatoes, boiled, peeled, and cubed
    3 Tbsp. vegetable oil
    ½ tsp. split urad dal
    1 tsp. black mustard seed
    2 dozen curry leaves
    1 large onion, chopped
    5 green chilies, finely sliced
    1 Tbsp. ginger, minced fine
    3 cloves garlic, chopped
    1 tsp. salt
    ½ tsp. ground turmeric

1. Heat oil in a large frying pan over medium; add urad dal, then mustard seeds, then curry leaves. Stir and fry for about thirty seconds.

2. Add the onion, green chilies, ginger, and garlic, and fry until golden-translucent.

3. Add salt and turmeric, stir for a few minutes more. Add the boiled potatoes and stir to combine, until they are well incorporated.

Spinach Pittu / Keerai Pittu

(30 minutes, serves 2–4)

This variation on pittu adds lovely green streaks of healthy spinach and sweet shallots for a savory base that could be eaten on its own—but will taste better with a nice sothi or curry (or both), and a little sambol. Cook in a pittu steamer if you have one handy (the shape mimics the bamboo it was originally cooked in), but any regular steamer should work fine.

> 2 cups plain flour
> ½ tsp. salt
> boiling water, as needed (I used about ½ cup)
> ¾ cup fresh spinach, chopped finely (thawed frozen chopped is also fine)
> ¼ cup grated coconut (if using desiccated, rehydrate with a Tbsp. of heated coconut milk)
> 1 green chili, chopped finely
> 1 shallot, chopped finely

1. Combine flours and salt in a bowl and microwave for one minute. Check if clumping, if not, microwave another minute or two, until it starts to clump. This process makes it easier to mix the flour with water in the next step without forming lumps. (Alternately, steam for a few minutes between two layers of cheesecloth, or roast the flour in a pan, or use pre-steamed or pre-roasted flour.)

2. Add boiling water to bowl, a little at a time, and stir with a wooden spoon—you're aiming for a texture similar to crumble or rough cornmeal, sometimes called pittu pebbles.

3. Stir in spinach, coconut, chili and onion, mixing well.

4. Fill steamer with mixture.

5. Steam in a large pot over simmering water for 10–15 minutes, until dough is thoroughly cooked. Push out onto a plate with a long wooden spoon and serve hot with curry and/or sambol.

Steamed Rice Cakes / Idli

(40 minutes + soaking and fermenting time, makes 36)

Soft, warm, slightly tangy idli fresh from the steamer are a healthy breakfast option (one-third lentil to two-thirds rice). Typically you'd use a specialty device, an idli steamer, but there are video tutorials online showing how to improvise an idli steamer with tin foil (with holes poked in it). You can also steam it as a flat cake and cut squares of it to serve, or steam it in oiled four ounce ramekins.

I admit, I mostly make idli from a just-add-water-and-oil mix, which uses baking soda as a rising agent and takes about twenty minutes. But if you want to go old-school and use actual fermentation (which supposedly has more health benefits), you can easily make it from scratch. You'll need to start about a day in advance of when you plan to serve. A great choice for a casual brunch, served with sambar and coconut chutney.

> 1 cup split urad dal
> 2 cups idli or parboiled rice
> 1 tsp. salt
> vegetable oil

1. In two bowls, soak dal and rice separately for eight hours. They will swell and expand notably, so leave room.

2. Drain rice and dal and grind both separately to a fine consistency. (A food processor will work fine.) Add water as needed; the ground rice will remain grainy, but should become a thick and pourable batter. The ground dal will turn into a dough on grinding.

3. Mix them together in a large bowl, using your clean hand to blend thoroughly. Add salt and mix in well.

4. Cover with a cloth and leave for eight hours or overnight to ferment. (In a cold climate, fermentation may not occur without a little help—I turn my oven on to 250°, and when it's reached temperature, turn it off and put the covered bowl in the oven to stay warm.)

5. Put some oil on a paper towel and grease the idli molds. Pour a spoonful of batter into each mold, filling them to the edge. Steam until they are cooked through, about 15–20 minutes; the idlis shouldn't be sticky to the touch; you're aiming for soft, but firm.

6. Remove from the mold and serve hot with coconut chutney and sambar.

Note: If you're having trouble with fermentation, adding a teaspoon of fenugreek to the batter will help.

Steamed Rice Flour and Coconut / Arisi-Maa Pittu

(20 minutes, serves 4–6)

Pittu is one of many dishes we eat instead of rice, at breakfast, lunch, or dinner; it's tastiest when made with fresh coconut, but works just fine with reconstituted desiccated coconut. With sambol and a little curry, it's a perfect breakfast. We would make this in a bamboo or metal cylinder steamer; you can improvise a cylindrical steamer by using a tall narrow can (about the size of a coffee can) and punching holes in the bottom. But pittu also works fine in any regular steamer; it just won't have the characteristic cylindrical shape when served. Traditionally, pittu was made solely with rice flour, but combining with wheat flour gives a softer texture.

    1 cup wheat flour
    1 cup white or red rice flour
    1 tsp. salt
    boiling water as needed (about half a cup)
    1 cup desiccated unsweetened coconut
    ¼ cup coconut milk

1. Combine flours and salt in a bowl and microwave for one minute. Check for clumping. If necessary, microwave another minute or two, until it starts to clump. This process makes it easier to mix the flour with water in the next step without forming lumps. (Alternatively, steam for a few minutes between two layers of cheesecloth, or roast the flour in a pan, or use pre-steamed or pre-roasted flour.)

2. Add boiling water to bowl, a little at a time, and stir with a wooden spoon—you're aiming for a texture similar to crumble or rough cornmeal, sometimes called pittu pebbles.

3. In a separate bowl, combine the desiccated coconut and coconut milk; work gently with your fingers until all the coconut is well-moistened (if you're using fresh or frozen grated coconut, you can skip this step, as it's ready to use).

4. Fill steamer with mixture, alternating thick layers of pittu pebbles and thin layers of coconut (or you can simply mix the coconut and pittu pebbles together before filling steamer); press it down lightly.

5. Steam in a large pot over boiling water for 10–15 minutes, until dough is thoroughly cooked. Push out onto a plate with a long wooden spoon and serve hot with curry and/or sambol and/or jaggery and coconut milk.

Steamed Rice Flour and Coconut with Milk / Pal Pittu

(20 minutes, serves 4–6)

Pal pittu follows a similar recipe to pittu, but the steamed flour is mixed with sweetened coconut milk for a soft, soothing breakfast. A gentle start to your day. This is also a nice way to use up leftover pittu.

> 1 cup wheat flour
> 1 cup white or red rice flour
> 1 tsp. salt
> boiling water as needed (about half a cup)
> 1 cup coconut milk
> 2 Tbsp. sugar

1. Combine flours and salt in a bowl and microwave for one minute. Check if clumping. If necessary, microwave another minute or two, until it starts to clump. This process makes it easier to mix the flour with water in the next step without forming lumps. (Alternatively, steam for a few minutes between two layers of cheesecloth, or roast the flour in a pan, or use pre-steamed or pre-roasted flour.)

2. Add boiling water to bowl, a little at a time, and stir with a wooden spoon—you're aiming for a texture similar to crumble or rough cornmeal, sometimes called pittu pebbles.

3. Fill steamer with pittu pebbles; press down lightly. Steam in a large pot over boiling water for 10–15 minutes, until dough is thoroughly cooked. Push out with a long wooden spoon and set aside.

4. In a small pot, bring remaining cup of coconut milk and sugar to a boil, then turn off heat. Add pittu and stir until milk is absorbed. Serve hot.

Stir-Fried Semolina / Uppuma

(20 minutes, serves 4–6)

When I was harried in grad school, I made a very fast, very simple version of this often—five minutes to boil water, add semolina with some vegan butter and salt, stir, and serve. Served with spicy jackfruit curry, it's a wonderful breakfast or dinner; the soft uppuma blends beautifully with the jackfruit—total comfort food.

This version, which is a little more time-consuming, offers more vegetables, more interesting seasonings, and a fluffier texture—it's tasty on its own, or with a vegetable curry. Both versions are great!

2 Tbsp. oil or vegan butter
1 onion, chopped fine
3 dried red chili pods
1 tsp. black mustard seed
1 tsp. cumin seed
1 stalk curry leaves
1 rounded tsp. salt
2 carrots chopped small
½ cup peas (or chopped green beans)
3 cups water
2 cups coarse semolina

1. Roast semolina in a dry pan over medium-high heat, stirring constantly for about five minutes, until it's darkened slightly. This will give the end result a fluffier texture, with less clumping. Remove to a plate and set aside.

2. Sauté onions with seasonings in oil or vegan butter on medium-high for a few minutes.

3. Add carrots and continue to cook until carrots are softened and onions are golden-translucent. Add peas and cook a few minutes longer.

4. Add water; bring to a boil.

5. Turn down to a simmer and quickly pour in the semolina, stirring constantly, making sure all the wheat is moistened. Remove from heat and allow dish to sit for a few minutes before serving. Serve warm.

Note: You can use farina (sold as Cream of Wheat) instead of semolina for an almost identical result. Semolina comes from durum wheat (high in protein, produces more gluten). Farina comes from any hard wheat but durum.

Stringhoppers / Idiyappam

(20–30 minutes, serves 4)

This is a classic Sri Lankan breakfast food: beautifully soft steamed rice flour noodles, deliciously comforting when served with a mild sothi and a bright pol sambol. Idiyappam also make a nice light dinner, often accompanied by a little curry; other appropriate accompaniments include luna miris or seeni sambol, ambulthiyal, or jaggery. Idiyappam take some effort to prepare, but when done right, there is nothing to match them, and cooks take pride in making the softest, fluffiest strings.

In Sri Lanka, idiyappam are made with both white rice flour and red rice flour. The heartier red rice flour has a little more flavor, but the white rice flour is gorgeously delicate; I can't pick a favorite. You can also buy 'idiyappam flour' already toasted and ready to go. If you have rice but no rice flour on hand, you can grind the rice yourself—in the old days, that would be done with a large mortar and pestle, but now an electric mill or coffee grinder will do the job, though you may need to run the flour through a fine sieve and re-grind portions until it is all of flour consistency. A thicker grain won't work for this preparation, as the dough won't be able to make its way through the tiny holes in the press. Wash the rice first, and spread it out on a clean dish towel to dry before grinding; generally thirty minutes should be sufficient.

Making idiyappam requires some specialized tools—you'll need a press, for one, with tiny holes to press the dough through. There are two basic kinds—one that you press down with both hands, and another that you crank; I find the latter notably easier, requiring less grip strength, though it does take a little practice to get the coordination down. They're both easily available online now, for around twenty dollars. (I tried using a potato ricer, but it didn't work well at all, and I don't think an Italian pasta maker would suffice either, though you could certainly try.) You also need a method for steaming the finished idiyappam—typically, you would use stringhopper mats designed for the purpose, though you can also steam them in an idli maker if you have one on hand, or on bamboo leaves.

When serving, it is best to eat this dish with your clean hand, so you can mix bites of idiyappam, sothi, and sambol together into little, perfect mouthfuls; eating with a fork will simply not give the tastiest results.

> 2 cups rice flour, white or red
> 1 tsp. salt
> 2 ½ cups boiling water, or as needed

1. Optional: Roast the flour in a dry pan over medium heat, stirring constantly, for five to eight minutes. This should improve the flavor slightly, and make the dough easier to work with; it's particularly useful in a humid climate, to prevent the flour from clumping as you work. It should be free-flowing, like salt, and the flour should not change color.

2. In the same pan or a large mixing bowl, stir in salt, and then add boiling water, a little at a time, mixing with a large wooden spoon. (Alternatively, this can be done in a stand mixer with the dough attachment; start slow so as not to spatter boiling water.) Continue adding water until it is starting to form a dough, then turn out onto a board and, as soon as it's cool enough to be worked, knead into a smooth dough. This is the trickiest part, and you may want to consult additional photos or videos online to get a sense of the correct consistency; it's hard to give exact measurements, since it's dependent on local humidity and other factors. The dough should be soft and not sticky; if it's hard, add a little more boiling water to soften it, and if it's sticky, add a little more rice flour (untoasted is fine).

3. Place the dough (you'll need to work in portions) in an idiyappam press and squeeze it onto idiyappam mats, using a circular motion to create the characteristic round nest of strings.

4. Place the idiyappam mats in a large steamer and steam 10–15 minutes, until the idiyappam are fully cooked; they should be springy in texture, but still soft. Remove from steamer and serve immediately with sothi and pol sambol.

Note: According to The Story of Our Food, *by Indian food historian K. T. Achaya, idiyappam has been around since at least the 1st century BCE.*

Stringhopper Biryani / Idiyappam Biryani

(30 minutes, serves 6)

This is a traditional Sri Lankan breakfast, and would be a lovely brunch option for guests. It looks a lot like fried rice, but has a notably lighter feel and flavor, and is full of healthy fresh veggies. Idiyappam biryani is gluten-free; you might add some canned chickpeas with the potatoes, to up the protein count.

Use whatever vegetables you have on hand—I happened to have fresh broccoli and frozen peas and corn, but carrots and chopped tomatoes are also very common, and add some nice color to the dish. Garnish with cashews and sultanas sautéed briefly in oil for a slightly fancier presentation.

This freezes well, so you can make a big batch and then save it to bring out for unexpected guests; just reheat with a sprinkling of water in the microwave. If you happen to have frozen idiyappam available in your grocery store, it works well thawed in this recipe.

- 1 onion, chopped fine
- ¼ cup vegetable oil
- 1 Tbsp. ginger, minced
- 3 cloves garlic , minced
- 1 serrano chili or 3 green chilies, chopped
- 1 tsp. cumin seed
- 1 tsp. black mustard seed
- 1 stalk curry leaves
- 1 tsp. ground turmeric
- 1 tsp. salt

1 potato, peeled and diced small
1 cup broccoli, chopped small
½ cup frozen peas
½ cup frozen corn
¼ cup chopped cilantro
1 tsp. lime juice
¼ cup coconut milk
12 idiyappam
cashews and sultanas cooked in oil, optional

1. Sauté onions in oil on medium-high with ginger, garlic, chilies, cumin seed, black mustard seed, and curry leaves for a few minutes, stirring, until onions are partially cooked.

2. Add turmeric, salt, and potato and keep cooking, stirring as needed to prevent sticking, until potatoes are mostly cooked, five to ten minutes.

3. Add broccoli, peas, corn, cilantro, and lime; keep stirring until thoroughly cooked, about five more minutes.

4. Finally, add coconut milk and mix to combine, then add in idiyappam and stir gently, trying not to break up the strands too much. Serve hot with pol sambol and/or vegan yogurt.

Tamarind Rice with Black Lentils

(10 minutes, serves 4)

Ever since I had children, I've become a little more focused on trying to get some protein into every meal, if possible. Lentils are protein powerhouses, and these lentils don't even require any soaking or boiling in advance—they just fry for a few minutes, and end up as crunchy little bites mixed in with the tangy tamarind rice. This rice is delicious with fried plantains, but to be honest, I often just eat it straight up, right out of the pot.

You can make fresh rice for this, but it's also a terrific way to revive day-old rice!

- 2 cups cooked rice
- 2 Tbsp. vegetable oil
- 1 Tbsp. urad dal (black lentil)
- ½ tsp. black mustard seed
- ½ tsp. fennel seed
- 4 dried red chilies
- 1 stalk (about a dozen) fresh curry leaves
- 1 Tbsp. cayenne
- 1 tsp. ground jaggery or brown sugar
- 1 tsp. salt
- ½ tsp. ground turmeric
- 6 Tbsp. tamarind juice (1 Tbsp. tamarind paste dissolved in 5 Tbsp. hot water)

NOTE: This recipe moves quickly, and it's worth having all the ingredients prepped in advance. You can measure out the whole spices into one container, and the ground spices into another, and dissolve the tamarind paste in advance.

1. Heat oil on medium-high and sauté lentil, mustard seed, cumin seed, dried chilies, curry leaves for two minutes, stirring constantly—be careful not to burn.

2. Stir in ground spices, then add tamarind juice. Bring to a boil and let simmer a few minutes, until thickened.

3. Remove from heat and stir in rice, mixing until well-blended. Serve hot!

Beverages

Beet Juice with Coconut Milk and Lime

Chai

Cocktails

Falooda

Mango Lassi

Mango-Passionfruit Punch or Mimosa

Fresh Sweet Lime Juice / Thesikkai Saaru

Spiced Yogurt Drink / Moru Thanni

Beet Juice with Coconut Milk and Lime

(10 mintes, serves 4)

I admit, vegetable juice drinks are new to me; I was a little suspicious when I first went to taste beet juice. I thought it might be very, well, beet-y.

But in fact, when you add cardamom, sugar, coconut, and most importantly, lime, the end result is a sweet and tangy drink packed full of nutrient goodness. This would be gorgeous in a pitcher on a brunch board, or served poolside.

- 1 large beet, peeled and cubed small
- 1 tsp. ground cardamom
- ¼–½ cup sugar (to taste)
- 2 cups coconut milk
- 2 cups water
- 3 Tbsp. lime juice

1. Combine ingredients in a blender; serve chilled.

Chai

(15 minutes, serves 4)

I've been delighted to see coffee shops across America start serving chai; as someone who for most of her adult life rarely drank coffee, it was lovely having other options. (I've recently become a coffee convert, mostly by necessity!) But I admit to often being disappointed in American coffeeshop chai—it's often made from powder, and is painfully grainy. And even when it's smooth, it's generally under-spiced and over-sweetened.

This is chai the way I like to make it when I'm feeling indulgent with myself; I vary the spices, and might also add peppercorns or nutmeg. Though I admit, most of the time at home, I just use Stash's ready-made Chai Tea bags, which are surprisingly tasty. I often have a cup of the decaf version at night, as I'm getting ready to go to bed, and then I sleep like a baby.

> 4 cups coconut milk or your favorite non-dairy milk
> 6 black Ceylon tea bags
> 2 2-inch cinnamon sticks
> 5 cloves
> 5 cardamom pods
> 5 slices fresh ginger
> jaggery or brown sugar to taste (about 2–4 tsp.)

1. In a saucepan, bring milk almost to a boil (but not quite).

2. Turn down heat and add tea, cinnamon, cloves, cardamom, and ginger. Simmer tea and spices in milk until well-brewed. The mixture should be aromatic and have a light-brown color.

3. Add sweetener to taste; stir until well blended.

4. Strain mixture through a fine sieve into four mugs. Serve hot.

Cocktails

Coconut arrack is the classic Sri Lankan hard liquor, made from the nectar of coconut flowers (not to be confused with the Middle Eastern arak, which is anise flavored, or the Indonesian arak, made from sugarcane). Traditional arrack is quite harsh, but recently more mellow versions have emerged, such as Mesh & Bone's Arakku, which is aged in halmilla (or Trincomalee maram) wood barrels. The flavor is somewhere between whiskey and bourbon.

I'm not a mixologist, so I have no precise amounts for you here—I tend to make cocktails more by feel. But these flavors go very well together, and you can adjust quantities to your taste. I'd recommend starting with about 1 ½–2 oz. of arrack per serving, and go from there.

Arrack Sour

arrack
ginger beer
fresh lime

Combine arrack and ginger beer in a highball glass filled with ice, add the juice of a lime, and garnish with a slice of lime.

Beetroot Cocktail

2 cups beets, peeled and roughly chopped
2 cups coconut milk
¼ cup sugar or jaggery
¼ cup lime juice
1 tsp. ground cinnamon
arrack

1. Combine beets, coconut milk, sugar or jaggery, lime juice, and cinnamon in blender and liquefy. (For a thinner cocktail, add up to 2 cups water.)

2. For each serving, stir 1–2 oz. arrack into ¾ cup juice. Serve cold.

Optional spicy variation: Some chopped green chili would go nicely with this!

Ceylon Sunrise

arrack
passionfruit puree
lime juice
crushed lemongrass

ginger beer

Combine arrack, passionfruit puree, lime juice, and lemongrass in a cocktail glass, top up with ginger beer, and serve garnished with lemongrass.

Planter's Tea

jaggery
hot black Ceylon tea
arrack
lime juice
cinnamon stick

Combine jaggery, hot tea, arrack, and lime juice in a punch glass, with a cinnamon stick to mix. Lovely for a holiday party, or if you're fighting a cold, or just to relax with in the late afternoon.

Serendib

arrack
jaggery
mango puree
fresh ginger, bruised
slices of mango
lime juice
ginger beer
mint leaves

Combine ingredients in a cocktail shaker, muddle well, and pour into large glass.

Falooda

(20 minutes, serves 4)

If you like boba tea, you should definitely try falooda. One of my mother's favorites, quite ridiculously pretty, and very cooling on a hot day.

>   agar-agar jelly, diced (see below)
>   3 cups white sugar
>   2 cups water
>   20 drops rose essence
>   1–2 tsp. liquid red food coloring
>   ice cold coconut milk or your favorite non-dairy milk as required, about 1 cup for each serving
>   crushed ice
>   wheat vermicelli (cooked 1" pieces), sago, or tapioca pearls (optional)
>   soaked tulsi or chia seeds (optional)
>   vegan ice cream, crushed pistachios or cashews, sultanas (optional)

Jelly:

>   3 cups water
>   4 rounded tsp. agar-agar powder or 1 cup soaked agar-agar strands
>   6 Tbsp. sugar
>   12 drops rose essence
>   1 tsp. liquid red food coloring
>   1 tsp. liquid green food coloring

1. Make syrup: Put sugar and water in a saucepan and cook over gentle heat until sugar dissolves. Cool. Add 20 drops rose essence and 1 teaspoon red coloring. You have now made rose syrup. Set aside.

2. Make rose jelly with agar-agar (which is vegetarian).

   If using agar-agar powder, measure water into a saucepan and sprinkle-powder over. If agar-agar strands are used, soak at least 2 hours in cold water, then drain and measure 1 cup loosely packed. Bring to a boil and simmer gently, stirring, until agar-agar dissolves. Powder takes about 10 minutes and the strands take longer, about 25–30 minutes. Add sugar and dissolve, remove from heat, cool slightly, and add 12 drops rose essence. Divide mixture between two large shallow dishes and color one red and the other green. Leave to set.

3. When jelly is quite cold and firm, cut with a sharp knife first into fine strips, then across into small dice.

4. Put about 2 tablespoons each of diced jelly and rose syrup into each tall glass, add vermicelli, sago, or tapioca pearls if desired. Fill up with ice-cold milk (pouring slowly over the back of a spoon to preserve layers) and crushed ice. Float some soaked tulsi or chia seeds on top if desired. Other toppings might include a quenelle of vegan vanilla ice cream, and/or some crushed pistachios or cashews, and/or some dried fruit, such as sultanas.

Mango Lassi

(10 minutes, serves 4)

Some people like their mango lassi very sweet; some like it hardly sweetened at all. It seems like that decision is best left up to the individual cook.

>　several ice cubes
>　1 cup vegan yogurt (more if desired)
>　1 jar (or 1 30 oz. can) fresh mango pieces or mango puree
>　1–2 drops of rose essence (careful not to add too much!)
>　3–5 cups iced water
>　¼ cup or more (or less) agave nectar or equivalent sweetener
>　chopped fruit as topping

1. Crush ice in blender.

2. Add yogurt, mango, and rose essence, and blend.

3. Add 3 cups water and blend—stop blender and taste, add more water if desired until preferred consistency is reached.

4. Add agave nectar to taste and blend; top with fruit and serve.

Mango-Passionfruit Punch or Mimosa

(10 minutes, serves 4)

For most parties, I'll make either the alcoholic or the non-alcoholic version of this. I'm afraid I never measure, so add ingredients to your taste! You can garnish with slices of lime if you're feeling fancy.

    mango juice
    passionfruit juice
    ginger ale or prosecco / champagne

Combine and enjoy!

Fresh Sweet Lime Juice / Thesikkai Saaru

(5 minutes, serves 2)

his refreshing drink is often served to guests on arrival, as they step out of the hot sun into the cool shelter of the home.

    4 limes
    2 cups water
    ½–1 tsp. salt
    2–4 tsp. sugar (to taste)

Squeeze juice from limes, add water, salt, and sugar. Serve cold.

Spiced Yogurt Drink / Moru Thanni

(15 minutes, serves 4)

n a hot day, this a wholesome way to cool down!

> 1 cup vegan yogurt (use your favorite; I like Culina, which is coconut milk based, but versions based on cashews would also work for this)
> ½ tsp. asafoetida powder / hing (optional)
> ½–2 tsp. salt (to taste)
> 3–4 cups water (to your desired drinking consistency)
> ½ red onion, chopped fine
> 1 green chili, chopped fine
> 1 tsp. cilantro, chopped fine
> 1 tsp. vegetable oil
> 1 tsp. black mustard seeds
> 1–2 Tbsp. lime juice (to taste)

1. In a large pouring container, mix yogurt with asafoetida powder (if using) and salt.

2. Add 2–4 cups water, stirring to combine, to your desired drinking consistency.

3. Add chopped onion, green chili, and cilantro to the beverage.

4. In a small pan on high, heat oil and add mustard seeds. When they start to splutter, remove from heat and add to the beverage, stirring to combine.

5. Add lime juice and adjust seasonings to taste. Serve cold as a refreshing beverage; it can also be served as an accompaniment to a rice meal, and in that instance, would be poured over the rice.

NOTE: To turn this into a refreshing cocktail, feel free to add a shot or two of arrack to the glass!

SWEETS

Coconut Rock / Coconut Ice

Kokis

Love Cake

Purple Yam Pudding or Porridge / Irasavalli Kizhangu Kanju

Rich Cake (Wedding / Christmas Cake)

Sesame Balls / Ellu Urundai / Thala Guli

Sweet Coconut Steamed Appams / Halapa

Sweet Thosai / Inippu Thosai

Tropical Fruit Salad with Ginger-Lime-Dressing

Tropical Fruit with Chili, Salt, and Lime

Coconut Rock / Coconut Ice

(15 minutes + cooling and cutting time, makes about 30)

This is a classic treat in Sri Lanka for holiday parties, school and church fairs, birthdays, etc. The colors make it perfect for an Easter or spring table, and it's popular with both children and adults.

The sweet seems to be more commonly referred to as coconut ice in the New Zealand / Australian Sri Lankan diaspora, and coconut rock elsewhere (though I haven't done an exhaustive study!).

There are various versions of this, including some that use desiccated coconut. My favorite version uses fresh coconut and rich coconut milk, for an end result that is both vegan and utterly delicious.

> 1 cup coconut milk
> 1 ½ lbs. sugar
> 1 lb. freshly grated coconut (thawed from frozen is fine)
> food coloring, if using

1. In a heavy medium saucepan, heat coconut milk and sugar on low, until sugar dissolves. Bring to a boil.

2. Add coconut and stir for another 5–7 minutes or so until the milk has mostly been reduced. (If you're using a candy thermometer, about 250°F, though this recipe doesn't require precision).

3. If you'd like multiple colors, divide into bowls. Color as desired; usually we'd leave some white and color another batch pink or green, to create a bicolor effect, but single colors also work fine, especially if you're going to make a few different batches.

4. Spread in a lightly oiled cookie sheet (or one layered with parchment paper), and flatten out using a lightly oiled spatula (or banana leaf, if you happen to have one on hand, and feel like going traditional). Layer additional layers immediately after, if using.

5. Allow to cool for a bit (at least 30 minutes), and then cut into squares or diamonds. If it seems sticky and hard to cut, let cool a little longer and try again; it shouldn't be difficult.

NOTE: For natural food colorings, I've used and would recommend both dragonfruit powder and saffron.

NOTE: Coconut rock will keep nicely in the fridge for weeks, or may be frozen for several months if needed.

Kokis

(30–45 minutes, serves several)

Kokis is a deep-fried, crispy treat made from rice flour and coconut milk. Although it's considered a traditional Sri Lankan dish, kokis is likely a result of Dutch colonial rule during the Kandyan period. Its name may have been derived from the Dutch word "koekjes," meaning cookies or biscuits.

Kokis is very similar to Swedish rosette cookies, and uses the same sort of rosette iron, but the use of rice flour and coconut milk gives a notably different result. Kokis may be made savory or sweet; they also resemble Persian nan panjereh, the achappam of Kerala, Mexican buñelos, and Portuguese filhós de forma.

Kokis are traditionally served for Sri Lankan (Sinhalese and Tamil) New Year celebrations in mid-April, along with kiri bath and other delicious sweetmeats. They're also popular at Christmas.

NOTE: To make kokis, you will need a special long-handled kokis iron / mold; in America, it may be easier to find if you search for a rosette iron / mold. Other popular shapes include stars and crossed wheels.

  1 ¼ cup rice flour
  ¾ cup coconut milk
  ¾ cup water
  2 Tbsp. sugar
  1 tsp. salt
  1 tsp. turmeric
  vegetable oil for deep frying

1. Combine the first six ingredients in a bowl, stirring to combine; you're aiming for something similar in consistency to thosai batter; it should lightly coat the back of a spoon.

2. Heat the oil over medium-high heat—if using an electric thermometer or fryer, aim for about 350°F degrees.

3. Dip mold in hot oil for a few seconds until it becomes hot (necessary to help the batter adhere properly).

4. Dip mold in batter, without immersing it completely—if you do, you won't be able to remove the kokis from the mold—and dip immediately in heated oil again.

5. After a few seconds, you can tap the mold against the side of the pan, and the kokis should slide off. If necessary, use a wooden (or metal) chopstick or skewer to help push the kokis off the mold. (It may be a little extra-sticky with a new mold.)

6. You can enjoy them as is (nice with a cup of sweet tea), sprinkle with powdered sugar, dip in a sugar syrup, or even dip in vegan chocolate and decorate. They will keep for about a week in a sealed container.

Savory variant: Omit sugar; mix in chili pepper flakes, black pepper, and curry leaves.

Love Cake

(2.5 hours, including baking time, serves dozens)

Some say this Portuguese-derived cake was baked to win the hearts of suitors, while others say it's because of the labor of love involved in all the cutting, chopping and grinding of the fruits, nuts, and spices (much easier these days with access to a food processor). But regardless, it tastes like love: sweet, tangy, and fragrant. My mother says it doesn't taste right without the crystallized pumpkin, which you can find at Indian grocery stores, though honestly, I like it just as well with the candied ginger. A perfect accompaniment to a cup of tea.

The vegan version uses beaten aquafaba to add lightness to the cake; if you haven't used aquafaba before, and are worried about your cake tasting of chickpeas—do not fret. There's no discernible chickpea flavor to the beaten aquafaba, especially once you fold it into a sweet batter.

- 8 oz. coconut oil, plus more for greasing
- 1 lb. raw unsalted cashews
- 14 oz. fine granulated sugar
- 5 very ripe bananas
- ½ cup aquafaba (water drained from a can of chickpeas)
- zest and juice of 2 limes (about 2–3 Tbsp. juice)
- zest of 1 orange
- 1 tsp. ground cinnamon
- ½ tsp. ground cardamom
- ¼ tsp. ground cloves
- ¼ tsp. ground nutmeg
- 3 drops rose water extract (or 2 tsp. rose water)
- 1 tsp. vanilla extract

12 oz. semolina, toasted

3 oz. candied ginger and/or crystallized pumpkin, minced as finely as possible

confectioners' sugar for dusting (optional)

1. Preheat the oven to 250°F. Classically, you would grease a 9×13 baking dish with coconut oil and line it with two layers of parchment paper, then grease the paper with coconut oil.

2. In food processor, grind cashews to coarse meal.

3. In a standing mixer (paddle attachment), beat ripe bananas and granulated sugar until creamy. Add zest, juice, spices, rosewater and vanilla; mix well.

4. Add semolina and mix well; add cashews and candied ginger / pumpkin and mix well.

5. In a separate bowl, beat aquafaba until stiff (about 12–15 minutes on high); fold gently into cake mixture.

6. Spoon batter into prepared pan; bake for 1 hour 30 minutes, until firm to the touch. Alternatively, spoon into greased and floured mini tea cake molds (Nordicware made the excellent one I used for this) and bake for about 50 minutes.

7. Let cool completely in the pan, dust with confectioner's sugar (optional), cut into squares and serve.

Purple Yam Pudding or Porridge / Irasavalli Kizhangu Kanji

(30 minutes, serves 4)

This is one of the prettiest Sri Lankan dishes—the color is sure to delight dinner guests and children. It's healthy too! Yams are good for you, and so is coconut milk; you can feel happy serving this dessert to one and all. Irasavalli is also often eaten for breakfast, in the same manner as a rice congee (or oatmeal).

Purple yam (*Dioscorea alata*), also known as ube (Philippines) or isu ewura (Nigeria), is native to Southeast Asia. It can be found fresh and frozen in your local Asian grocery stores.

    2 cups purple yams, peeled and diced
    2 cups coconut milk
    1 cup water
    ¼ cup sugar
    1 Tbsp. lime juice
    pinch of salt
    1 drop rose essence, or pinch of ground cardamom (optional)

1. In a saucepan, combine yams, coconut milk, and water. Bring to a boil and cook ten minutes, stirring occasionally, until yams are cooked through.

2. Remove from heat and either mash with the back of a wooden spoon, or use a blender (an immersion blender makes it easy) to puree the yam and combine it with the coconut milk.

3. When well blended, return to heat, add remaining ingredients, and simmer 10–15 minutes more, stirring, until pudding is thick and starting to pull away from the sides of the pan.

4. Serve hot, with your choice of garnishes—ripe banana, ripe mango, coconut flakes are all good options.

NOTE: If you're using frozen yams, they may have lost some color in the freezing process. If the purple is not sufficiently purple for your delight, do feel free to add a drop or two of food coloring.

Rich Cake (Wedding / Christmas Cake)

(30–60 minutes chopping time + 3 hr baking time + cooling time, serves dozens)

Americans are often scared of fruitcake. There's a massive cultural myth that fruitcake is some horrid dry thing that gets pressed upon you by similarly dried-up aunts. But a real fruitcake, the kind that's related to a traditional British steamed figgy pudding, is dense, rich, moist, fruity, and pleasantly alcoholic.

The chopping is labor-intensive (and would gum up a food processor), so I'd recommend having a few friends over to help and rewarding them with slabs of fruitcake to take home. (Note the long baking time, though!) Traditionally, you would use glacé cherries and other candied fruit, but Kevin doesn't like them, so we stick to just dried fruit in ours.

- 2 ½ lbs. mixed dried fruit (not pineapple)
- 8 oz. candied ginger (if you like it—if not, just use more dried fruit)
- 1 lb. jam (I use a mix of whatever's in the fridge)
- 2–4 oz. mixed peel (optional)
- 8 oz. raw cashews (or blanched almonds)
- ¼ cup brandy (with more for pouring later)
- 12 oz. vegan butter or solid coconut oil
- 1 lb. powdered sugar
- 5 very ripe bananas (from frozen is fine)
- 2 tsp. grated lemon rind
- ½ tsp. ground cardamom
- 1 tsp. ground cinnamon

1 tsp. grated nutmeg
¾ tsp. ground cloves
2 Tbsp. vanilla extract
1 Tbsp. almond extract
2 tsp. rose extract
8 oz. fine semolina
½ cup aquafaba (chickpea water from can)
Almond paste (optional)

1. Oil and flour a 9x12 cake pan or two 8x8 cake pans.

2. Chop dried fruit, mixed peel, and nuts finely. Combine fruits, nuts, and jam in large bowl, sprinkle with brandy, stir, cover, and leave while mixing cake. This can be done the day before, allowing the fruit more time to soak in the brandy.

3. Preheat oven to 275°F. In the biggest bowl you have, cream vegan butter or solid oil and sugar until light. Add very ripe bananas one at a time, beating well. Add grated rind, spices, and flavorings and mix well. Add semolina and beat until well combined, then mix in fruit (easiest done with your clean hand).

4. Whip aquafaba until stiff and, using a wooden spoon, gently fold (as best you can) through thick, stiff mixture. Turn into prepared cake pan(s), cover edges lightly in foil, and bake in 275°F oven for 2.5–3 hours until cooked through in center—cover the cake with foil after the first hour to prevent over-browning.

5. Cool completely, preferably overnight, then remove paper and wrap cake in plastic wrap; if you like, you can sprinkle a few more tablespoons of brandy over the cold cake before wrapping it. Chill in refrigerator (or other cool place) for at least a month. Every week or so, you can unwrap it, add more brandy, and rewrap it, if you like that sort of thing.

6. Alternatively, ice the cake with almond paste and then cut the cake into small rectangles (about two fingers wide) and wrap each individually in wax paper and colored foil—this is the presentation we would use for weddings, where little girls would carry baskets of the cake around at the end of the wedding and give a little cake to each guest to take home.

NOTE: This cake can be kept in an airtight tin for a year or longer. It just gets better and better—I recommend making it no later than mid-November if you want to serve it at Christmas.

Sesame Balls / Ellu Urundai / Thala Guli

(30–45 minutes, makes many)

Delicious little balls of sesame seeds + coconut + date + jaggery—great as a dessert, at tea time, or just a nibble to power you through your day. Traditionally in Jaffna, these were often made with just sesame seeds and jaggery, perhaps with a little rice flour / water as a binder, but I find them much tastier with the addition of coconut and dates.

> 1 cup white sesame seeds
> 1 cup desiccated coconut
> ½–1 cup chopped dates
> 1 cup jaggery or dark brown sugar

1. Toast sesame seeds and coconut on medium-low heat, stirring, until the coconut turns light tan. Don't toast for too long, or the sesame seeds will become bitter.

2. Let cool, then pound all the ingredients together or combine in food processor until you can form the mixture into balls that hold together. You may need to adjust the amount of dates (Medjool dates tend to be moister), and/or add a little water.

3. Shape into small balls, squeezing mixture together firmly. Enjoy!

NOTE: These may be stored refrigerated for a few weeks. For most recipes, I'd recommend fresh coconut or rehydrating desiccated, and you certainly can, but these will actually keep longer if you skip the rehydrating phase.

Sweet Coconut Steamed Appams / Halapa

(1 hour, makes several)

I first encountered a version of this recipe titled "Ooda Appam" in a Jaffna-based cookbook, but had trouble finding other recipes under that name. With the help of one of my cousins and Sri Lankan friends, I realized this was essentially halapa, which made my search for recipes much easier.

To make halapa, you need pani pol, a mix of sweetener (usually jaggery and/or kithul treacle) and coconut. Sometimes, pani pol serves as a filling to the rice flour steamed bun, but in this version, the pani pol is mixed directly in with the toasted rice flour.

In Sri Lanka, the flattened balls would traditionally be steamed in kenda leaves, but those are hard to find in America; you can use banana leaves or parchment paper. These are best right out of the steamer—be careful not to burn your fingers or tongue when devouring them! Delicious with a cup of tea; also commonly served for breakfast with fresh fruit.

> 1 cup red rice flour
> 1 cup grated fresh coconut
> ¾ cup jaggery or dark brown sugar
> ½ tsp. salt
> hot water
> 1 banana leaf (or a few sheets of parchment paper)
> 1 tsp. vegetable oil

1. In a dry pan, toast rice flour, stirring, until aromatic.

2. In a large bowl, combine rice flour, coconut, jaggery, and salt to a smooth paste; add a little hot water as needed to bring together.

3. Briefly run hot water on the banana leaf to soften it, and cut it into pieces (roughly 2x2 inches); alternately, use squares of parchment paper.

4. Use a paper towel dipped in the vegetable oil to grease each piece of banana leaf (parchment paper).

5. Make small balls from the paste, then place each ball on the center of a leaf. Flatten into a circular shape and fold the leaf over.

6. Steam over simmering water in a covered steamer until cooked, about 15–20 minutes. Serve warm.

Sweet Thosai / Inippu Thosai

(30 minutes + 3 hours, serves 16)

Coconut, jaggery, and brown sugar are mixed together to make a sweet filling for this crepe-like pancake. Traditionally it would have been made with rice flour; but now wheat flour is often used, which gives a softer result. You could also try a half and half mix of rice flour and wheat flour.

> 3 ½ cups all-purpose flour
> 1 tsp. baking powder
> ¼ tsp. salt
> water as needed (about 2 ½ cups)
> 2 cups fresh grated (or reconstituted desiccated) coconut
> ½ cup grated jaggery
> ½ cup brown sugar

1. Mix first four ingredients, using enough water to make a thick pancake batter.

   Note: Traditionally, you would set the batter aside for three hours at this point, but if you proceed directly to step 2, you'll still get a good result.

2. In a separate bowl, combine grated coconut, jaggery, and brown sugar; using your clean hand will allow you break up any lumps of jaggery or sugar and mix them thoroughly.

3. Stir batter again, and add a little more water to make a thinner, pourable batter.

4. Heat a small frying pan on high, grease lightly. Pour a little mixture into the pan (about ½ cup) and smooth into a circle; cook for a few minutes, until the bottom turns light golden. You can flip if you want, but there is generally no need.

5. Remove to a plate and place about a teaspoon of coconut mixture in a line down the center. (You can start the next thosai cooking at this point, so that you're alternating making thosai and filling them for maximum efficiency—or, you can make all the thosai first, covering them with a kitchen towel to keep them warm, and then fill them.) Roll the thosai relatively tightly to make a small, neat roll. Serve warm—a lovely tiffin snack for children, or with your afternoon tea.

Note: These thosai are also yummy wrapped around a little eggplant sambol, for a savory option. A nice little party appetizer.

Tropical Fruit Salad with Ginger-Lime Dressing

The key component of this salad is the ripe avocado—not a typical fruit salad component in America, but I assure you, delicious. I first had it at the Pinnawela Elephant Orphanage, where visitors meet and feed milk to little baby elephants. I ate it at a restaurant that overlooked the river where the elephants came to bathe, and the ladies all held black parasols above their heads, to protect their complexion from the sun's rays.

This fruit salad is yummy straight up, or served over vegan vanilla ice cream. Fruits used may include mango, papaya, starfruit, lychee, rambutan, jackfruit, passionfruit, pineapple, banana, and more...

> 1 lime
> 2 Tbsp. agave or other sweet syrup
> 2 Tbsp. fresh ginger, minced
> 4 cups fruit for salad
> 1 avocado

1. For dressing, combine the first three ingredients in a small saucepan and simmer ten minutes or so, covered. Let cool. Can be made in advance and refrigerated.

2. Cut up desired fruit (if using jackfruit, you may want to oil hands first) and mix with dressing. Serve and enjoy!

Tropical Fruit with Chili, Salt, and Lime

An alternate fruit salad, for those who like a little more kick. This is my absolute favorite, made with perfectly ripe mango, and is ideal to enjoy on the beach, graced by sun and waves. A little taste of island life.

Cut up fruit (see previous for suggestions) and season with salt, cayenne, and fresh lime juice, to taste. I like about ¼ teaspoon cayenne, ¼ teaspoon salt, and ½ lime for 1 cup fruit. Serves lots.

After-Dinner Digestive

A little bowl of fennel or anise seeds and rock sugar makes a lovely finish to the meal. Your guests can just spoon themselves a little bit into their palms and pop it directly in their mouths. There are brightly-colored candy-coated versions available in South Asian grocery stores and online.

ACKNOWLEDGEMENTS

This book is deeply indebted to all my readers, on Facebook and elsewhere, who offered advice, encouragement, test cooking, and demands for more recipes. It wouldn't exist without you—thank you more than I can say. Kickstarter supporters—in the challenging world of modern publishing, you made this book possible!

I've always dreamed of having a small press; this is the first book fully published by my Serendib House team, and I think they did a splendid job. Stephanie Bailey, my editor, did meticulous and thoughtful work, with invaluable contributions from Emmanuel Henderson, Darius Vinesar, and Ethan Yeung. Look, folks—we made a book! Hopefully with many more books to come...

Thanks to my designer Jeremy John Parker, to contributing photographers Paul Goyette and Suchetha Wijenayake, and to illustrator Pamudu Tennakoon, for making this book beautiful, bringing all my words to gorgeous life. Suchetha—thank you so much for being my generous guide to Sri Lanka whenever I visit; you helped me find my way home again, and helped introduce my daughter to her homeland. We'll always remember that visit to Mt. Lavinia beach.

Particular thanks to vegan and vegetarian friends and acquaintances who taste-tested my food, test-cooked my recipes, and offered a wealth of helpful suggestions; I would have been lost without you, especially Swati Saxena!

Appreciation as well to friends and family who have been eating my food for decades, not hesitating to offer constructive criticism along with the compliments. *This is good, but maybe a little more lime juice next time?* You made these dishes better. Special thanks to Aaron Lav, who answered food science questions, and to Kat Tanaka Okopnik and my sweetie, Jed Hartman, who have given exceptional feedback over the years. The best feedback, of course, is watching them clean their plates and come back for seconds.

Jed has also supported me and this project in a myriad of ways, including helping me and Kavi get to Sri Lanka in December 2018; the trip wouldn't have been possible without him, and the book would have been the poorer for it. You make everything better, sweetie.

Cultural cooking gratitude to my Sri Lankan friends and relatives who answered questions from their own memories and experience cooking—my sisters, Mirna and Sharmila Mohanraj, and friends Samanthi Hewakapuge, Suchetha Wijenayake, Sugi Ganeshananthan, Mythri Jegathesan, Rozanne Arulanandam, Elaine and Angeline Martyn, and all the rest. Talented cooks all. (Any remaining culture errors are my own.)

Most of all, to Roshani Anandappa, most excellent of friends, who has shared meals and ardent cooking discussions (not quite arguments!) with me for decades now. Someday, I swear, we'll open that Chicagoland Sri Lankan restaurant, or at least host some pop-up dinners. It's going to be fun!

Thanks as well to my aunties, exceptional cooks, all. For all the times you insisted on my taking away another stuffed-full bag of rolls and patties as I headed to the airport, I'm grateful. You'll never know how much pleasure they brought.

Deep gratitude to my parents—to my mother, Jacintha Mohanraj, for her incredible cooking, of course, but also to my father, Navaratnasingam Mohanraj, who was always ready to provide a mini-lecture on Sri Lankan Tamil culture and the beauty of our language. It can be challenging for any immigrant, maintaining a connection to homeland culture in the diaspora, but my parents always did their best to help us stay connected. I'm planning to take another stab at Tamil classes someday soon.

Finally, I must thank Kevin, for all the reasons, but mostly for the many days and nights when he cooked separate meals for the children, because they were suspicious of Amma's spicy food, especially once she'd started experimenting. Often Kavi and Anand would taste what I made, but teaching them to love the vast range of Sri Lankan dishes is an ongoing process. It's getting better as they get older, but in the meantime, it's a good thing Daddy can cook.

Best of men, best of husbands.

AUTHOR BIOGRAPHY

Mary Anne Mohanraj is author of *Bodies in Motion* (HarperCollins), *A Feast of Serendib* (Mascot Books), and fourteen other titles. *Bodies in Motion* was a finalist for the Asian American Book Awards, a *USA Today* Notable Book, and has been translated into six languages. She's recipient of two Illinois Arts Council Fellowships, and has received a Locus Award and a Breaking Barriers Award from the Chicago Foundation for Women.

Mohanraj is Clinical Associate Professor of fiction and literature at the University of Illinois at Chicago, serves as Executive Director of DesiLit (desilit.org), and directs the Kriti Festival of Art and Literature (kritifestival.org). She founded and served for ten issues as editor-in-chief of *Jaggery*, a South Asian literary journal (jaggerylit.com). She runs the Oak Park Area Garden Club Facebook group—she loves incorporating garden harvests into her recipes—has served on the Oak Park library board, and was recently elected to the Oak Park D200 school board.

Mohanraj was born in Sri Lanka in 1971, and moved to America at the age of two. When she was young, her family would go back often to visit grandparents and other relatives, until the war intervened. Since peace returned, Mohanraj has started travelling back to Sri Lanka more often for research and pleasure. She would love to develop a food tour and writing retreat to be held on the island.

When she's not cooking, Mohanraj is writing science fiction and superhero stories; recent books include *The Stars Change* (Sri Lankans in space), and stories for George R.R. Martin's *Wild Cards* anthology series. Forthcoming titles include *Jump Space*, the reissue of *Perennial*, and a cancer memoir. She lives in a creaky old Victorian in Oak Park, just outside Chicago, with her partner, Kevin, two children, and assorted animals.

WWW.SERENDIBKITCHEN.COM | WWW.MARYANNEMOHANRAJ.COM

ILLUSTRATOR BIOGRAPHY

Pamudu Tennakoon, born and raised in Sri Lanka, is currently a first-year Ph.D student in History of Art and Architecture at Brown University. Prior to commencing her studies at Brown University, Pamudu received her B.A from Bryn Mawr College, where she majored in Growth and Structure of Cities and Fine Arts (Sculpture), and her MPhil from the School of Architecture at the University of Queensland. Her academic work focuses on colonial architecture, particularly the contemporary understandings and usages of colonial architecture. Her artistic works, on the other hand, questions the line between natural and man-made. Inspired by her previous work with wire, she is currently exploring the language of three dimensional wire drawing within two dimensional line drawing.

மீண்டும் சந்திப்போம்

meendum santhipom
we'll meet again

Index

A

Achar / Spicy Pineapple Pickle 145
After-Dinner Digestive 234
agar-agar
  Falooda 208
  Spices and Ingredients 12
agave nectar
  Mango Lassi 210
  Tropical Fruit Salad with Ginger-Lime Dressing 232
Alcohol:
  arrack 205, 206, 207
  champagne 211
  ginger beer 205, 206, 207
  prosecco 211
all-purpose flour
  Hibiscus (Shoeflower) Curry / Sembaruthipoo Kari 52
  Millet Roti, with Coconut and Jaggery / Kurakkan Roti 174
  Plain Roti / Kothambu Roti 178
  Sweet Thosai / Inippu Thosai 230
almond extract
  Rich Cake (Wedding / Christmas Cake) 224
almond paste
  Rich Cake (Wedding / Christmas Cake) 224
almonds, blanched
  Rich Cake (Wedding / Christmas Cake) 224
anise seeds
  After-Dinner Digestive 234
anise, star
  Spiced Tomato Jam / Thakkaali Yaam 149
Appam / Hoppers 165
Appams, Sweet Coconut Steamed / Halapa 228
apple cider vinegar. *See* vinegar, apple cider
apples, green
  Green Tomato Chutney with Apples 120
aquafaba
  Hibiscus (Shoeflower) Curry / Sembaruthipoo Kari 52
  Love Cake 220
  Rich Cake (Wedding / Christmas Cake) 224
Arisi-Maa Pittu / Steamed Rice Flour and Coconut 188
arrack
  Arrack Sour 205
  Beetroot Cocktail 206
  Ceylon Sunrise 206
  Planter's Tea 207
  Serendib 207
Arrack Sour 205
asafoetida powder / hing
  Spiced Yogurt Drink / Moru Thanni 213
asparagus
  Asparagus Poriyal 69
Asparagus Poriyal 69
avocado
  Tropical Fruit Salad with Ginger-Lime Dressing 232

B

baker's sugar. *See* sugar, fine
baking powder
  Hoppers / Appam 165
  Plain Roti / Kothambu Roti 178
  Sweet Thosai / Inippu Thosai 230
baking soda
  Bonda 104
  Kundu Thosai / Paniyaram 169
balsamic vinegar. *See* vinegar, balsamic
banana leaf
  Sweet Coconut Steamed Appams / Halapa 228
bananas, green
  Spicy Plantain Curry 65
bananas, very ripe
  Love Cake 220
  Rich Cake (Wedding / Christmas Cake) 224

Beet Curry 31
Beet Juice with Coconut Milk and Lime 202
Beetroot Cocktail 206
beets
  Beet Curry 31
  Beet Juice with Coconut Milk and Lime 202
  Beetroot Cocktail 206
  Pickled Beet Salad 114
besan / chickpea flour. *See* chickpea flour / besan
Biryani 162
bitter gourd
  Bitter Gourd Sambol / Paavakkai Sambol 124
  Bitter Gourd Sambol / Paavakkai Sambol 124
black pepper
  Biryani 162
  Broccoli Varai 85
  Lime-Masala Mushrooms 89
  Marinated Ginger-Garlic Seitan 91
  Vegetable and Lentil Stew / Sambar 96
black pepper, ground
  Cabbage Varai / Muttaikoss Varai 87
  Coriander Soup / Kothamalli Rasam 154
  Cucumber Salad 113
  Cucumber-Tomato Raita 146
  Fried Garlic Curry / Poritha Ulli Kari 42
  Green Bean Varai 88
  Herbal Porridge / Kola Kenda 158
  Vegetable Cutlets 111
black pepper, whole
  Spiced Tomato Jam / Thakkaali Yaam 149
  Spices and Ingredients 16
  Spicy Pineapple Pickle / Achar 145
Bonda 104
bottle gourd
  Bottle Gourd and Spinach Curry 32
  Milk Rice / Kiri Bath 172
Bottle Gourd and Spinach Curry 32
brandy
  Rich Cake (Wedding / Christmas Cake) 224

breadcrumbs, dry
  Vegetable Cutlets 111
Brinjal Moju / Eggplant Pickle 136
broccoli
  Broccoli Varai 85
  Stringhopper Biryani / Idiyappam Biryani 197
Broccoli Varai 85
brown sugar
  Chai 203
  Chili-Mango Cashews / Kari-Maangai Kaaju 106
  Cranberry-Rhubarb Chutney 117
  Eggplant Curry / Kaththarikkai Kari 38
  Eggplant, Plantain, and Potato Curry / Kaliya Kari 40
  Ginger Sambol / Injii Sambol 129
  Green Tomato Chutney with Apples 120
  Kundu Thosai / Paniyaram 169
  Marinated Ginger-Garlic Tempeh 92
  Millet Roti, with Coconut and Jaggery / Kurakkan Roti 174
  Roasted Brussels Sprouts with Jaggery, Balsamic, and Cayenne 94
  Sesame Balls / Ellu Urundai / Thala Guli 227
  Spiced Tomato Jam / Thakkaali Yaam 149
  Sri Lankan Roasted Pumpkin Seeds 156
  Sweet Coconut Steamed Appams / Halapa 228
  Sweet Thosai / Inippu Thosai 230
  Tamarind Rice with Black Lentils 199
brussels sprouts
  Brussels Sprouts Poriyal 71
  Roasted Brussels Sprouts with Jaggery, Balsamic, and Cayenne 94
Brussels Sprouts Poriyal 71
Brussels Sprouts, Roasted, with Jaggery, Balsamic, & Cayenne 94
butter, vegan
  Chili-Mango Cashews / Kari-Maangai Kaaju 106
  Golden Rice Pilaf 164
  Jaggery Pongal / Sakkarai Pongal 167

Lime-Masala Mushrooms 89
Rich Cake (Wedding / Christmas Cake) 224
Stir-Fried Semolina / Uppuma 192

C

cabbage
  Cabbage Varai / Muttaikoss Varai 87
Cabbage Varai / Muttaikoss Varai 87
cardamom, ground
  Beet Juice with Coconut Milk and Lime 202
  Jaggery Pongal / Sakkarai Pongal 167
  Kundu Thosai / Paniyaram 169
  Love Cake 220
  Purple Yam Pudding or Porridge / Irasavalli Kizhangu Kanji 222
  Rich Cake (Wedding / Christmas Cake) 224
cardamom pods
  Biryani 162
  Chai 203
  Eggplant, Plantain, and Potato Curry / Kaliya Kari 40
  Spiced Tomato Jam / Thakkaali Yaam 149
  Spices and Ingredients 12
  Sweet Onion Sambol / Seeni Sambol 134
cardamom seeds
  Master Recipe: Sri Lankan Curry Powder 18
Carrot Curry 34
carrots
  Carrot Curry 34
  Chopped Roti Stir-Fry / Kottu Roti 179
  Quick-Pickled Cucumber-Carrot Relish 143
  Stir-Fried Semolina / Uppuma 192
  Vegetable and Lentil Stew / Sambar 96
Cashew Curry / Kaju Kari 35
cashews
  Biryani 162
  Cashew Curry / Kaju Kari 35
  Chili-Mango Cashews / Kari-Maangai Kaaju 106
  Falooda 208
  Golden Rice Pilaf 164
  Jaggery Pongal / Sakkarai Pongal 167
  Stringhopper Biryani / Idiyappam Biryani 197
Cashews, Chili-Mango / Kari-Maankai Kaju 106
cashews, raw unsalted
  Love Cake 220
  Rich Cake (Wedding / Christmas Cake) 224
cauliflower
  Cauliflower Poriyal 73
Cauliflower Poriyal 73
cayenne
  Asparagus Poriyal 69
  Bottle Gourd and Spinach Curry 32
  Chili-Mango Cashews / Kari-Maangai Kaaju 106
  Chili Onion Sambol / Lunu Miris Sambol 125
  Coconut Sambol / Thengai-Poo or Pol Sambol 126
  Deviled Potatoes / Urulai Kizhangu 67
  Eggplant Pickle / Brinjal Moju 136
  Eggplant, Plantain, and Potato Curry / Kaliya Kari 40
  Green Jackfruit Curry / Palakkai Kari 48
  Green Tomato Chutney with Apples 120
  Jaffna Whole Eggplant Fry / Yaalpana Kaththarikaii Poriyal 77
  Leeks Fried with Chili 147
  Lime Pickle 138
  Mango Pickle / Maangai Oorukkai 141
  Marinated Ginger-Garlic Seitan 91
  Marinated Ginger-Garlic Tofu 90
  Master Recipe: Sri Lankan Curry Powder 18
  Ripe Jackfruit Curry / Palapazham Kari 63
  Roasted Brussels Sprouts with Jaggery, Balsamic, and Cayenne 94
  Spices and Ingredients 12
  Spicy Pineapple Pickle / Achar 145
  Spicy Plantain Curry 65
  Stir-fried Chickpea Snack / Kadalai Sundal 109

Sweet Onion Sambol / Seeni Sambol 134
Tamarind Rice with Black Lentils 199
Tempered Potatoes 83
Tropical Fruit with Chili, Salt, and Lime 233
Ceylon Sunrise 206
Chai 203
champagne
  Mango-Passionfruit Punch or Mimosa 211
chia seeds
  Falooda 208
chickpea flour / besan
  Bonda 104
  Marinated Ginger-Garlic Seitan 91
  Stir-fried Chickpea Snack / Kadalai Sundal 109
  Vegetable Cutlets 111
chickpeas
  Stir-fried Chickpea Snack / Kadalai Sundal 109
Chickpea Snack, Stir-fried / Kadalai Sundal 109
Chili-Mango Cashews / Kari-Maankai Kaju 106
Chili Onion Sambol / Lunu Miris Sambol 125
chives
  Marinated Ginger-Garlic Tofu 90
Chopped Roti Stir-Fry / Kottu Roti 179
Christmas / Wedding Cake (Rich Cake) 224
Chutney, Cranberry Rhubarb 117
Chutney, Green Coconut / Thengai Chutney 119
Chutney, Green Tomato, with Apples 120
Chutney, Mango-Ginger 122
cilantro
  Coriander Soup / Kothamalli Rasam 154
  Green Tomato and Lentil Curry 50
  Marinated Ginger-Garlic Tofu 90
  Spiced Yogurt Drink / Moru Thanni 213
  Stringhopper Biryani / Idiyappam Biryani 197
cinnamon, ground
  Beetroot Cocktail 206
  Green Mango Curry / Mankkai Kari 46
  Love Cake 220
  Rich Cake (Wedding / Christmas Cake) 224
cinnamon stick
  Biryani 162
  Broccoli Varai 85
  Cashew Curry / Kaju Kari 35
  Chai 203
  Coconut Milk Gravy / Sothi 152
  Cranberry-Rhubarb Chutney 117
  Curried Pumpkin Soup 156
  Eggplant, Plantain, and Potato Curry / Kaliya Kari 40
  Green Tomato and Lentil Curry 50
  Green Tomato Chutney with Apples 120
  Hibiscus (Shoeflower) Curry / Sembaruthipoo Kari 52
  Master Recipe: Sri Lankan Curry Powder 18
  Planter's Tea 207
  Ripe Jackfruit Curry / Palapazham Kari 63
  Spices and Ingredients 12
  Sweet Onion Sambol / Seeni Sambol 134
  Tempered Lentils (Paruppu) 81
  Tempered Potatoes 83
cloves, ground
  Love Cake 220
  Rich Cake (Wedding / Christmas Cake) 224
  Spices and Ingredients 13
cloves, whole
  Biryani 162
  Chai 203
  Eggplant, Plantain, and Potato Curry / Kaliya Kari 40
  Green Tomato Chutney with Apples 120
  Master Recipe: Sri Lankan Curry Powder 18
  Spiced Tomato Jam / Thakkaali Yaam 149
  Spices and Ingredients 13
  Sweet Onion Sambol / Seeni Sambol 134
Cocktails 205
coconut, desiccated
  Sesame Balls / Ellu Urundai / Thala Guli 227

coconut, desiccated unsweetened
  Coconut Sambol / Thengai-Poo or Pol Sambol 126
  Spinach Pittu / Keerai Pittu 184
  Steamed Rice Flour and Coconut / Arisi-Maa Pittu 188
coconut, fresh grated
  Coconut Rock / Coconut Ice 216
  Dried Hibiscus Poriyal 74
  Ginger Sambol / Injii Sambol 129
  Green Coconut Chutney / Thengai Chutney 119
  Kundu Thosai / Paniyaram 169
  Millet Roti, with Coconut and Jaggery / Kurakkan Roti 174
  Rose (or Hibiscus) Salad / Rosappu Pachadi 115
  Rose Sambol 133
  Spinach Pittu / Keerai Pittu 184
  Sweet Coconut Steamed Appams / Halapa 228
  Sweet Thosai / Inippu Thosai 230
coconut, frozen grated
  Coconut Rock / Coconut Ice 216
  Green Coconut Chutney / Thengai Chutney 119
Coconut Ice / Coconut Rock 216
coconut milk
  Beet Curry 31
  Beet Juice with Coconut Milk and Lime 202
  Beetroot Cocktail 206
  Bottle Gourd and Spinach Curry 32
  Carrot Curry 34
  Cashew Curry / Kaju Kari 35
  Chai 203
  Coconut Milk Gravy / Sothi 152
  Coconut Rock / Coconut Ice 216
  Cucumber Salad 113
  Curried Pumpkin Soup 156
  Deviled Potatoes / Urulai Kizhangu 67
  Dried Hibiscus Poriyal 74
  Drumstick Curry / Murungakkai Kari 36
  Eggplant Curry / Kaththarikkai Kari 38
  Eggplant, Plantain, and Potato Curry / Kaliya Kari 40
  Eggplant Sambol / Kaththarikkai Sambol 128
  Falooda 208
  Fried Garlic Curry / Poritha Ulli Kari 42
  Green Chili Curry / Kari-Milaggai Kari 44
  Green Coconut Chutney / Thengai Chutney 119
  Green Jackfruit Curry / Palakkai Kari 48
  Green Mango Curry / Maankai Kari 46
  Green Tomato and Lentil Curry 50
  Herbal Porridge / Kola Kenda 158
  Hibiscus (Shoeflower) Curry / Sembaruthipoo Kari 52
  Hoppers / Appam 165
  Jaggery Pongal / Sakkarai Pongal 167
  Kokis 218
  Mild Green Plantain Curry 55
  Milk Rice / Kiri Bath 172
  Okra Curry / Vendikkai Kari 57
  Pineapple Curry, with Coconut Milk and Saffron 59
  Pumpkin Curry 61
  Purple Yam Pudding or Porridge / Irasavalli Kizhangu Kanji 222
  Red Rice Congee 176
  Spices and Ingredients 15
  Spicy Plantain Curry 65
  Steamed Rice Flour and Coconut / Arisi-Maa Pittu 188
  Steamed Rice Flour and Coconut with Milk / Pal Pittu 190
  Stringhopper Biryani / Idiyappam Biryani 197
  Tempered Lentils / Paruppu 81
Coconut Milk Gravy / Sothi 152
coconut milk, thick
  Biryani 162
  Ripe Jackfruit Curry / Palapazham Kari 63
coconut oil
  Golden Rice Pilaf 164
  Love Cake 220
coconut oil, solid

Rich Cake (Wedding / Christmas Cake) 224
Coconut Rock / Coconut Ice 216
Coconut Sambol / Thengai-Poo, or Pol Sambol 126
coconut, shredded unsweetened
  Broccoli Varai 85
  Cabbage Varai / Muttaikoss Varai 87
  Green Bean Varai 88
  Kale Sambol 130
  Spices and Ingredients 13
confectioners' sugar. *See* sugar, confectioners'
coriander, ground
  Biryani 162
coriander leaf. *See* cilantro
coriander seeds
  Coriander Soup / Kothamalli Rasam 154
  Master Recipe: Sri Lankan Curry Powder 18
  Spices and Ingredients 13
Coriander Soup / Kothamalli Rasam 154
corn, frozen
  Stringhopper Biryani / Idiyappam Biryani 197
cranberries
  Cranberry-Rhubarb Chutney 117
Cranberry Rhubarb Chutney 117
crushed red pepper flakes
  Cranberry-Rhubarb Chutney 117
cucumber
  Bottle Gourd and Spinach Curry 32
  Cucumber Salad 113
  Cucumber-Tomato Raita 146
  Milk Rice / Kiri Bath 172
  Quick-Pickled Cucumber-Carrot Relish 143
Cucumber Salad 113
Cucumber-Tomato Raita 146
cumin, ground
  Biryani 162
  Coriander Soup / Kothamalli Rasam 154
cumin, whole
  Asparagus Poriyal 69
  Beet Curry 31

Bottle Gourd and Spinach Curry 32
Broccoli Varai 85
Brussels Sprouts Poriyal 71
Carrot Curry 34
Cashew Curry / Kaju Kari 35
Cauliflower Poriyal 73
Deviled Potatoes / Urulai Kizhangu 67
Dried Hibiscus Poriyal 74
Eggplant Curry / Kaththarikkai Kari 38
Eggplant, Potato, and Pea Pod Poriyal 75
Green Jackfruit Curry / Palakkai Kari 48
Green Tomato and Lentil Curry 50
Lentil Patties / Kadalai Vadai 107
Master Recipe: Sri Lankan Curry Powder 18
Master Recipe: Sri Lankan Seasoned Onions 20
Mixed Vegetable Poriyal 79
Okra Curry / Vendikkai Kari 57
Pickled Beet Salad 114
Pineapple Curry, with Coconut Milk and Saffron 59
Pumpkin Curry 61
Spices and Ingredients 13
Stir-Fried Semolina / Uppuma 192
Stringhopper Biryani / Idiyappam Biryani 197
Vegetable Cutlets 111
Curried Pumpkin Soup 156
Curry, Beet 31
Curry, Bottle Gourd and Spinach 32
Curry, Carrot 34
Curry, Cashew / Kaju Kari 35
Curry, Drumstick / Murungakkai Kari 36
Curry, Eggplant / Kaththarikkai Kari 38
Curry, Eggplant, Plantain, and Potato / Kaliya Kari 40
Curry, Fried Garlic / Poritha Ulli Kari 42
Curry, Green Chili / Kari Milaggai Kari 44
Curry, Green Jackfruit / Palakkai Kari 48
Curry, Green Mango / Maankai Kari 46
Curry, Green Tomato and Lentil 50
Curry, Hibiscus (Shoeflower) / Sembaruthipoo Kari 52

curry leaves
  Asparagus Poriyal 69
  Beet Curry 31
  Biryani 162
  Bitter Gourd Sambol / Paavakkai Sambol 124
  Broccoli Varai 85
  Cashew Curry / Kaju Kari 35
  Coconut Milk Gravy / Sothi 152
  Coriander Soup / Kothamalli Rasam 154
  Eggplant Curry / Kaththarikkai Kari 38
  Eggplant, Potato, and Pea Pod Poriyal 75
  Green Coconut Chutney / Thengai Chutney 119
  Lentil Patties / Kadalai Vadai 107
  Mango Pickle / Maankai Oorukkai 141
  Masala Potato Filling 182
  Pineapple Curry, with Coconut Milk and Saffron 59
  Pumpkin Curry 61
  Spices and Ingredients 13
  Tempered Lentils / Paruppu 81
  Tempered Potatoes 83
curry leaves, dried
  Master Recipe: Sri Lankan Curry Powder 18
curry leaves, on stalk
  Bonda 104
  Bottle Gourd and Spinach Curry 32
  Chopped Roti Stir-Fry / Kottu Roti 179
  Dried Hibiscus Poriyal 74
  Drumstick Curry / Murungakkai Kari 36
  Eggplant, Plantain, and Potato Curry / Kaliya Kari 40
  Fried Garlic Curry / Poritha Ulli Kari 42
  Green Mango Curry / Maankai Kari 46
  Green Tomato and Lentil Curry 50
  Jaffna Whole Eggplant Fry / Yaalpana Kaththarikaii Poriyal 77
  Lime Pickle 138
  Mild Green Plantain Curry 55
  Red Rice Congee 176
  Ripe Jackfruit Curry / Palapazham Kari 63
  Spicy Plantain Curry 65
  Stir-Fried Semolina / Uppuma 192
  Stringhopper Biryani / Idiyappam Biryani 197
  Sweet Onion Sambol / Seeni Sambol 134
  Tamarind Rice with Black Lentils 199
  Vegetable and Lentil Stew / Sambar 96
Curry, Mild Green Plantain 55
Curry, Okra / Vendikkai Kari 57
Curry, Pineapple, with Coconut Milk and Saffron 59
curry powder. *See* Sri Lankan Curry Powder
Curry Powder, Sri Lankan, Master Recipe 18
Curry, Pumpkin 61
Curry, Ripe Jackfruit / Palapazham Kari 63
Curry, Spicy Plantain 65
Cutlets, Vegetable 111

D

dates
  Cranberry-Rhubarb Chutney 117
  Sesame Balls / Ellu Urundai / Thala Guli 227
Deviled Potatoes / Urulai Kizhangu 67
Dried Hibiscus Poriyal 74
dried red chilies. *See* red chilis, dried
Drumstick Curry / Murungakkai Kari 36
drumsticks
  Vegetable and Lentil Stew / Sambar 96
drumsticks, fresh or frozen
  Drumstick Curry / Murungakkai Kari 36
dry mustard. *See* mustard powder

E

eggplant
  Biryani 162
  Eggplant Curry / Kaththarikkai Kari 38
  Eggplant Pickle / Brinjal Moju 136
  Eggplant, Plantain, and Potato Curry / Kaliya Kari 40
  Eggplant, Potato, and Pea Pod Poriyal 75
  Eggplant Sambol / Kaththarikkai Sambol 128
  Jaffna Whole Eggplant Fry / Yaalpana Kaththarikaii Poriyal 77
  Vegetable and Lentil Stew / Sambar 96

Eggplant Curry / Kaththarikkai Kari 38
Eggplant Pickle / Brinjal Moju 136
Eggplant, Plantain, and Potato Curry / Kaliya Kari 40
Eggplant, Potato, and Pea Pod Poriyal 75
Eggplant Sambol / Kaththarikkai Sambol 128
eggplants, Japanese
    Eggplant, Potato, and Pea Pod Poriyal 75
    Vegetable and Lentil Stew / Sambar 96
egg replacer. *See* aquafaba
Ellu Urundai / Thala Guli / Sesame Balls 227

F

Falooda 208
fennel seeds
    After-Dinner Digestive 234
    Asparagus Poriyal 69
    Fried Garlic Curry / Poritha Ulli Kari 42
    Green Chili Curry / Kari-Milaggai Kari 44
    Green Tomato Chutney with Apples 120
    Lentil Patties / Kadalai Vadai 107
    Lime Pickle 138
    Master Recipe: Sri Lankan Curry Powder 18
    Quick-Pickled Cucumber-Carrot Relish 143
    Spices and Ingredients 14
    Tamarind Rice with Black Lentils 199
fenugreek seed
    Bottle Gourd and Spinach Curry 32
    Coconut Milk Gravy / Sothi 152
    Drumstick Curry / Murungakkai Kari 36
    Fried Garlic Curry / Poritha Ulli Kari 42
    Green Chili Curry / Kari-Milaggai Kari 44
    Green Tomato and Lentil Curry 50
    Lime Pickle 138
    Master Recipe: Sri Lankan Curry Powder 18
    Mild Green Plantain Curry 55
    Okra Curry / Vendikkai Kari 57
    Pumpkin Curry 61
    Savory Rice Pancakes / Thosai 181

Spices and Ingredients 14
Spicy Plantain Curry 65
filling, potatoes
    Masala Potato Filling 182
fingerhot chilis. *See* green chilis, fingerhot
flowers, hibiscus
    Dried Hibiscus Poriyal 74
    Hibiscus (Shoeflower) Curry / Sembaruthipoo Kari 52
    Rose (or Hibiscus) Salad / Rosappu Pachadi 115
flowers, marigold petals
    Curried Pumpkin Soup 156
flowers, roses
    Rose (or Hibiscus) Salad / Rosappu Pachadi 115
    Rose Sambol 133
fresh coriander. *See* cilantro
Fresh Sweet Lime Juice / Thesikkai Saaru 212
Fried Garlic Curry / Poritha Ulli Kari 42
fruit, fresh
    Mango-Ginger Chutney 122
    Mango Lassi 210
    Tropical Fruit Salad with Ginger-Lime Dressing 232
    Tropical Fruit with Chili, Salt, and Lime 233
fruit, mixed dried
    Rich Cake (Wedding / Christmas Cake) 224
Fruit Salad, Tropical, with Ginger-Lime Dressing 232
Fruit, Tropical, with Chili, Salt, and Lime 233

G

Garlic Curry, Fried / Poritha Ulli Kari 42
garlic, fresh
    Asparagus Poriyal 69
    Bottle Gourd and Spinach Curry 32
    Brussels Sprouts Poriyal 71
    Drumstick Curry / Murungakkai Kari 36
    Eggplant Pickle / Brinjal Moju 136

   Eggplant, Plantain, and Potato Curry /
      Kaliya Kari 40
   Eggplant, Potato, and Pea Pod Poriyal 75
   Green Jackfruit Curry / Palakkai Kari 48
   Green Mango Curry / Maankai Kari 46
   Mango Pickle / Maankai Oorukkai 141
   Masala Potato Filling 182
   Master Recipe: Sri Lankan Seasoned
      Onions 20
   Okra Curry / Vendikkai Kari 57
   Pineapple Curry, with Coconut Milk and
      Saffron 59
   Pumpkin Curry 61
   Red Rice Congee 176
   Roasted Brussels Sprouts with Jaggery,
      Balsamic, and Cayenne 94
   Stringhopper Biryani / Idiyappam Biryani
      197
   Tempered Potatoes 83
   Vegetable and Lentil Stew / Sambar 96
garlic powder
   Marinated Ginger-Garlic Seitan 91
   Marinated Ginger-Garlic Tempeh 92
   Marinated Ginger-Garlic Tofu 90
garlic, whole cloves
   Bottle Gourd and Spinach Curry 32
   Coriander Soup / Kothamalli Rasam 154
   Fried Garlic Curry / Poritha Ulli Kari 42
   Green Coconut Chutney / Thengai
      Chutney 119
   Lentil Patties / Kadalai Vadai 107
ginger ale
   Mango-Passionfruit Punch or Mimosa 211
ginger beer
   Arrack Sour 205
   Ceylon Sunrise 206
   Serendib 207
ginger, candied
   Love Cake 220
   Rich Cake (Wedding / Christmas Cake)
      224
ginger, fresh
   Asparagus Poriyal 69
   Brussels Sprouts Poriyal 71

   Chai 203
   Cranberry-Rhubarb Chutney 117
   Drumstick Curry / Murungakkai Kari 36
   Eggplant Pickle / Brinjal Moju 136
   Eggplant, Plantain, and Potato Curry /
      Kaliya Kari 40
   Eggplant, Potato, and Pea Pod Poriyal 75
   Ginger Sambol / Injii Sambol 129
   Green Coconut Chutney / Thengai
      Chutney 119
   Green Jackfruit Curry / Palakkai Kari 48
   Green Mango Curry / Maankai Kari 46
   Green Tomato Chutney with Apples 120
   Lentil Patties / Kadalai Vadai 107
   Mango-Ginger Chutney 122
   Mango Pickle / Maankai Oorukkai 141
   Masala Potato Filling 182
   Master Recipe: Sri Lankan Seasoned
      Onions 20
   Pineapple Curry, with Coconut Milk and
      Saffron 59
   Pumpkin Curry 61
   Red Rice Congee 176
   Serendib 207
   Stringhopper Biryani / Idiyappam Biryani
      197
   Tropical Fruit Salad with Ginger-Lime
      Dressing 232
   Vegetable and Lentil Stew / Sambar 96
ginger powder
   Marinated Ginger-Garlic Seitan 91
   Marinated Ginger-Garlic Tempeh 92
   Marinated Ginger-Garlic Tofu 90
   Ginger Sambol / Injii Sambol 129
golden raisins. *See* sultanas
Golden Rice Pilaf 164
green beans
   Chopped Roti Stir-Fry / Kottu Roti 179
   Green Bean Varai 88
   Stir-Fried Semolina / Uppuma 192
   Vegetable and Lentil Stew / Sambar 96
Green Bean Varai 88
Green Chili Curry / Kari Milaggai Kari 44
green chilies

Asparagus Poriyal 69
Beet Curry 31
Bitter Gourd Sambol / Paavakkai Sambol 124
Bonda 104
Bottle Gourd and Spinach Curry 32
Broccoli Varai 85
Cabbage Varai / Muttaikoss Varai 87
Chopped Roti Stir-Fry / Kottu Roti 179
Coconut Milk Gravy / Sothi 152
Cucumber Salad 113
Cucumber-Tomato Raita 146
Drumstick Curry / Murungakkai Kari 36
Eggplant, Potato, and Pea Pod Poriyal 75
Eggplant Sambol / Kaththarikkai Sambol 128
Fried Garlic Curry / Poritha Ulli Kari 42
Ginger Sambol / Injii Sambol 129
Green Chili Curry / Kari-Milaggai Kari 44
Green Coconut Chutney / Thengai Chutney 119
Green Mango Curry / Maankai Kari 46
Jaffna Whole Eggplant Fry / Yaalpana Kaththarikaii Poriyal 77
Kundu Thosai / Paniyaram 169
Lentil Patties / Kadalai Vadai 107
Mango Pickle / Maankai Oorukkai 141
Masala Potato Filling 182
Pineapple Curry, with Coconut Milk and Saffron 59
Pumpkin Curry 61
Quick-Pickled Cucumber-Carrot Relish 143
Red Rice Congee 176
Rose (or Hibiscus) Salad / Rosappu Pachadi 115
Spiced Yogurt Drink / Moru Thanni 213
Spices and Ingredients 14
Spinach Pittu / Keerai Pittu 184
Stringhopper Biryani / Idiyappam Biryani 197
Vegetable Cutlets 111
green chilies, fingerhot
   Eggplant Pickle / Brinjal Moju 136
Hibiscus (Shoeflower) Curry / Sembaruthipoo Kari 52
Mild Green Plantain Curry 55
Plantain Sambol 131
Spices and Ingredients 14
Spicy Plantain Curry 65
Green Coconut Chutney / Thengai Chutney 119
green grams / mung bean, toasted
   Jaggery Pongal / Sakkarai Pongal 167
Green Jackfruit Curry / Palakkai Kari 48
Green Mango Curry / Maankai Kari 46
Green Tomato and Lentil Curry 50
Green Tomato Chutney with Apples 120

H

Halapa / Sweet Coconut Steamed Appams 228
Herbal Porridge / Kola Kenda 158
herbs, fresh
   Herbal Porridge / Kola Kenda 158
hibiscus flowers
   Dried Hibiscus Poriyal 74
   Hibiscus (Shoeflower) Curry / Sembaruthipoo Kari 52
   Rose (or Hibiscus) Salad / Rosappu Pachadi 115
Hibiscus Poriyal, Dried 74
Hibiscus (Shoeflower) Curry / Sembaruthipoo Kari 52
hing / asafoetida powder
   Spiced Yogurt Drink / Moru Thanni 213
Hoppers / Appam 165

I

ice cream, vegan
   Falooda 208
idiyappam
   Stringhopper Biryani / Idiyappam Biryani 197
Idiyappam Biryani / Stringhopper Biryani 197
Idiyappam / Stringhoppers 194

idli
  Savory Rice Pancakes / Thosai 181
  Spices and Ingredients 14
  Steamed Rice Cakes / Idli 186
Idli / Steamed Rice Cakes 186
Inippu Thosai / Sweet Thosai 230
Injii Sambol / Ginger Sambol 129
Irasavalli Kizhangu Kanji / Purple Yam
    Pudding or Porridge 222

J

jackfruit, fresh green
  Biryani 162
  Green Jackfruit Curry / Palakkai Kari 48
jackfruit, ripe
  Ripe Jackfruit Curry / Palapazham Kari 63
Jaffna Whole Eggplant Fry / Yaalpana
    Kaththarikaii Poriyal 77
jaggery
  Beetroot Cocktail 206
  Chai 203
  Chili-Mango Cashews / Kari-Maangai
      Kaaju 106
  Cranberry-Rhubarb Chutney 117
  Eggplant, Plantain, and Potato Curry /
      Kaliya Kari 40
  Ginger Sambol / Injii Sambol 129
  Green Tomato Chutney with Apples 120
  Herbal Porridge / Kola Kenda 158
  Hoppers / Appam 165
  Jaggery Pongal / Sakkarai Pongal 167
  Kundu Thosai / Paniyaram 169
  Marinated Ginger-Garlic Tempeh 92
  Millet Roti, with Coconut and Jaggery /
      Kurakkan Roti 174
  Planter's Tea 207
  Red Rice Congee 176
  Roasted Brussels Sprouts with Jaggery,
      Balsamic, and Cayenne 94
  Serendib 207
  Sesame Balls / Ellu Urundai / Thala Guli
      227
  Spiced Tomato Jam / Thakkaali Yaam 149
  Spices and Ingredients 15

Sweet Coconut Steamed Appams / Halapa
    228
Sweet Thosai / Inippu Thosai 230
Tamarind Rice with Black Lentils 199
Jaggery Pongal / Sakkarai Pongal 167
jam
  Rich Cake (Wedding / Christmas Cake)
      224
Jam, Spiced Tomato / Thakkaali Yaam 149
juice, lemon. *See* lemon juice
juice, lime. *See* lime juice
juice, mango. *See* mango juice
juice, passionfruit. *See* passionfruit juice

K

Kadalai Sundal / Stir-fried Chickpea Snack
    109
Kadalai Vadai / Lentil Patties 107
Kaju Kari / Cashew Curry 35
kale
  Kale Sambol 130
Kale Sambol 130
Kaliya Kari / Eggplant, Plantain, and Potato
    Curry 40
Kari-Maankai Kaju / Chili-Mango Cashews
    106
Kari Milaggai Kari / Green Chili Curry 44
Kaththarikkai Kari / Eggplant Curry 38
Kaththarikkai Sambol / Eggplant Sambol
    128
Keerai Pittu / Spinach Pittu 184
ketchup
  Deviled Potatoes / Urulai Kizhangu 67
  Green Jackfruit Curry / Palakkai Kari 48
  Spices and Ingredients 15
Kiri Bath / Milk Rice (with Bottle Gourd
    Variation) 172
Kokis 218
Kola Kenda / Herbal Porridge 158
Kothamalli Rasam / Coriander Soup 154
Kothambu Roti / Roti, Plain 178
Kottu Roti / Roti Stir-Fry, Chopped 179
Kundu Thosai / Paniyaram 169
Kurakkan Roti / Millet Roti, with Coconut
    and Jaggery 174

L

leeks
   Chopped Roti Stir-Fry / Kottu Roti 179
   Leeks Fried with Chili 147
Leeks Fried with Chili 147
leftover curry
   Chopped Roti Stir-Fry / Kottu Roti 179
lemongrass, crushed
   Ceylon Sunrise 206
   Spices and Ingredients 15
lemon juice
   Spiced Tomato Jam / Thakkaali Yaam 149
lemon rind, grated
   Rich Cake (Wedding / Christmas Cake) 224
lemon rind, strips
   Tempered Lentils / Paruppu 81
lemon zest
   Spiced Tomato Jam / Thakkaali Yaam 149
Lentil Patties / Kadalai Vadai 107
lentils, black. *See* urad dal, split
lentils, mung, split
   Green Tomato and Lentil Curry 50
lentils, red
   Lentil Patties / Kadalai Vadai 107
   Tempered Lentils / Paruppu 81
   Vegetable and Lentil Stew / Sambar 96
Lentils, Tempered / Paruppu 81
lime juice
   Asparagus Poriyal 69
   Beet Curry 31
   Beet Juice with Coconut Milk and Lime 202
   Bonda 104
   Bottle Gourd and Spinach Curry 32
   Broccoli Varai 85
   Cashew Curry / Kaju Kari 35
   Ceylon Sunrise 206
   Chili Onion Sambol / Lunu Miris Sambol 125
   Coconut Milk Gravy / Sothi 152
   Coconut Sambol / Thengai-Poo or Pol Sambol 126
   Cucumber Salad 113
   Curried Pumpkin Soup 156
   Eggplant, Potato, and Pea Pod Poriyal 75
   Eggplant Sambol / Kaththarikkai Sambol 128
   Ginger Sambol / Injii Sambol 129
   Green Chili Curry / Kari-Milaggai Kari 44
   Green Coconut Chutney / Thengai Chutney 119
   Green Jackfruit Curry / Palakkai Kari 48
   Hibiscus (Shoeflower) Curry / Sembaruthipoo Kari 52
   Jaffna Whole Eggplant Fry / Yaalpana Kaththarikaii Poriyal 77
   Kale Sambol 130
   Lime-Masala Mushrooms 89
   Lime Pickle 138
   Love Cake 220
   Marinated Ginger-Garlic Seitan 91
   Marinated Ginger-Garlic Tempeh 92
   Marinated Ginger-Garlic Tofu 90
   Mild Green Plantain Curry 55
   Planter's Tea 207
   Purple Yam Pudding or Porridge / Irasavalli Kizhangu Kanji 222
   Ripe Jackfruit Curry / Palapazham Kari 63
   Rose Sambol 133
   Serendib 207
   Spiced Yogurt Drink / Moru Thanni 213
   Spices and Ingredients 15
   Spicy Plantain Curry 65
   Stir-fried Chickpea Snack / Kadalai Sundal 109
   Stringhopper Biryani / Idiyappam Biryani 197
   Tempered Potatoes 83
   Tropical Fruit with Chili, Salt, and Lime 233
Lime-Masala Mushrooms 89
Lime Pickle 138
limes
   Arrack Sour 205
   Fresh Sweet Lime Juice / Thesikkai Saaru 212
   Lime Pickle 138

Tropical Fruit Salad with Ginger-Lime Dressing 232
lime zest
  Cranberry-Rhubarb Chutney 117
  Love Cake 220
Love Cake 220
Lunu Miris Sambol / Chili Onion Sambol 125

M

Maankai Kari / Green Mango Curry 46
Maankai Oorukkai / Mango Pickle 141
mangoes, green
  Green Mango Curry / Maankai Kari 46
  Stir-fried Chickpea Snack / Kadalai Sundal 109
mangoes, ripe
  Mango-Ginger Chutney 122
  Mango Lassi 210
  Mango Pickle / Maankai Oorukkai 141
  Serendib 207
Mango-Ginger Chutney 122
mango juice
  Mango-Passionfruit Punch or Mimosa 211
Mango Lassi 210
Mango-Passionfruit Punch or Mimosa 211
Mango Pickle / Maankai Oorukkai 141
mango puree
  Mango Lassi 210
  Serendib 207
mango slices, dried
  Chili-Mango Cashews / Kari-Maangai Kaaju 106
marigold petals
  Curried Pumpkin Soup 156
Marinated Ginger-Garlic Tofu (with Seitan and Tempeh Variations) 90
masoor dal
  Lentil Patties / Kadalai Vadai 107
Master Recipe: Sri Lankan Curry Powder 18
Master Recipe: Sri Lankan Seasoned Onions 20
methi seed. *See* fenugreek seed
Mild Green Plantain Curry 55

milk, coconut. *See* coconut milk
milk, non-dairy
  Chai 203
Milk Rice / Kiri Bath (with Bottle Gourd Variation) 172
millet flour
  Millet Roti, with Coconut and Jaggery / Kurakkan Roti 174
Millet Roti, with Coconut and Jaggery / Kurakkan Roti 174
Mimosa or Mango-Passionfruit Punch 211
mint leaves
  Ginger Sambol / Injii Sambol 129
  Rose (or Hibiscus) Salad / Rosappu Pachadi 115
  Serendib 207
Mixed Vegetable Poriyal 79
mixed vegetables, fresh or frozen and thawed
  Vegetable Cutlets 111
Moru Thanni / Spiced Yogurt Drink 213
mung bean, toasted / green grams
  Jaggery Pongal / Sakkarai Pongal 167
Murungakkai Kari / Drumstick Curry 36
mushrooms
  Biryani 162
  Lime-Masala Mushrooms 89
  Vegetable and Lentil Stew / Sambar 96
Mushrooms, Lime-Masala 89
mustard, ground
  Eggplant Pickle / Brinjal Moju 136
mustard seeds
  Bottle Gourd and Spinach Curry 32
  Dried Hibiscus Poriyal 74
  Eggplant, Potato, and Pea Pod Poriyal 75
  Fried Garlic Curry / Poritha Ulli Kari 42
  Green Mango Curry / Maankai Kari 46
  Masala Potato Filling 182
  Pumpkin Curry 61
  Spices and Ingredients 12
  Tempered Potatoes 83
  Vegetable and Lentil Stew / Sambar 96
mustard seeds, black
  Asparagus Poriyal 69
  Beet Curry 31
  Bonda 104

Broccoli Varai 85
Brussels Sprouts Poriyal 71
Carrot Curry 34
Cashew Curry / Kaju Kari 35
Cauliflower Poriyal 73
Coriander Soup / Kothamalli Rasam 154
Deviled Potatoes / Urulai Kizhangu 67
Eggplant Curry / Kaththarikkai Kari 38
Green Bean Varai 88
Green Jackfruit Curry / Palakkai Kari 48
Green Tomato and Lentil Curry 50
Green Tomato Chutney with Apples 120
Lime Pickle 138
Mango Pickle / Maankai Oorukkai 141
Master Recipe: Sri Lankan Seasoned Onions 20
Mixed Vegetable Poriyal 79
Okra Curry / Vendikkai Kari 57
Pineapple Curry, with Coconut Milk and Saffron 59
Spiced Yogurt Drink / Moru Thanni 213
Spices and Ingredients 12
Stir-Fried Semolina / Uppuma 192
Stringhopper Biryani / Idiyappam Biryani 197
Tamarind Rice with Black Lentils 199
Vegetable Cutlets 111
mustard seeds, black or brown
  Plantain Sambol 131
  Quick-Pickled Cucumber-Carrot Relish 143
  Spices and Ingredients 12
Muttaikoss Varai / Cabbage Varai 87

N

nutmeg, grated
  Rich Cake (Wedding / Christmas Cake) 224
nutmeg, ground
  Love Cake 220

O

okra
  Okra Curry / Vendikkai Kari 57

Vegetable and Lentil Stew / Sambar 96
Okra Curry / Vendikkai Kari 57
onions
  Asparagus Poriyal 69
  Beet Curry 31
  Biryani 162
  Bonda 104
  Broccoli Varai 85
  Brussels Sprouts Poriyal 71
  Cabbage Varai / Muttaikoss Varai 87
  Carrot Curry 34
  Cashew Curry / Kaju Kari 35
  Cauliflower Poriyal 73
  Chili Onion Sambol / Lunu Miris Sambol 125
  Coconut Milk Gravy / Sothi 152
  Coconut Sambol / Thengai-Poo or Pol Sambol 126
  Cucumber Salad 113
  Deviled Potatoes / Urulai Kizhangu 67
  Dried Hibiscus Poriyal 74
  Drumstick Curry / Murungakkai Kari 36
  Eggplant Curry / Kaththarikkai Kari 38
  Eggplant, Plantain, and Potato Curry / Kaliya Kari 40
  Eggplant, Potato, and Pea Pod Poriyal 75
  Eggplant Sambol / Kaththarikkai Sambol 128
  Fried Garlic Curry / Poritha Ulli Kari 42
  Green Bean Varai 88
  Green Chili Curry / Kari-Milaggai Kari 44
  Green Coconut Chutney / Thengai Chutney 119
  Green Jackfruit Curry / Palakkai Kari 48
  Green Mango Curry / Maankai Kari 46
  Green Tomato and Lentil Curry 50
  Green Tomato Chutney with Apples 120
  Hibiscus (Shoeflower) Curry / Sembaruthipoo Kari 52
  Kale Sambol 130
  Kundu Thosai / Paniyaram 169
  Lentil Patties / Kadalai Vadai 107
  Masala Potato Filling 182
  Master Recipe: Sri Lankan Seasoned Onions 20

Mixed Vegetable Poriyal 79
Okra Curry / Vendikkai Kari 57
Pumpkin Curry 61
Quick-Pickled Cucumber-Carrot Relish 143
Red Rice Congee 176
Ripe Jackfruit Curry / Palapazham Kari 63
Stir-Fried Semolina / Uppuma 192
Stringhopper Biryani / Idiyappam Biryani 197
Sweet Onion Sambol / Seeni Sambol 134
Tempered Lentils / Paruppu 81
Tempered Potatoes 83
Vegetable Cutlets 111
onions, pearl
 Eggplant Pickle / Brinjal Moju 136
 Stir-fried Chickpea Snack / Kadalai Sundal 109
onions, red
 Bitter Gourd Sambol / Paavakkai Sambol 124
 Bottle Gourd and Spinach Curry 32
 Chopped Roti Stir-Fry / Kottu Roti 179
 Cranberry-Rhubarb Chutney 117
 Ginger Sambol / Injii Sambol 129
 Mild Green Plantain Curry 55
 Pineapple Curry, with Coconut Milk and Saffron 59
 Rose (or Hibiscus) Salad / Rosappu Pachadi 115
 Rose Sambol 133
 Spiced Yogurt Drink / Moru Thanni 213
 Spicy Plantain Curry 65
 Vegetable and Lentil Stew / Sambar 96
Onions, Seasoned, Master Recipe 20
orange zest
 Love Cake 220

p

Paavakkai Sambol / Bitter Gourd Sambol 124
Palakkai Kari / Green Jackfruit Curry 48
Palapazham Kari / Ripe Jackfruit Curry 63
Pal Pittu / Steamed Rice Flour and Coconut with Milk 190

pandan leaf
 Eggplant, Plantain, and Potato Curry / Kaliya Kari 40
 Spices and Ingredients 16
Paniyaram / Kundu Thosai 169
paprika
 Coconut Sambol / Thengai-Poo or Pol Sambol 126
Paruppu / Tempered Lentils 81
passionfruit juice
 Mango-Passionfruit Punch or Mimosa 211
passionfruit puree
 Ceylon Sunrise 206
Patties, Lentil / Kadalai Vadai 107
pea pods
 Eggplant, Potato, and Pea Pod Poriyal 75
peas
 Stir-Fried Semolina / Uppuma 192
peas, frozen
 Stringhopper Biryani / Idiyappam Biryani 197
peel, mixed
 Rich Cake (Wedding / Christmas Cake) 224
peppercorns. See black pepper, whole
Pickled Beet Salad 114
Pickle, Eggplant / Brinjal Moju 136
Pickle, Lime 138
Pickle, Mango / Maankai Oorukkai 141
Pickle, Spicy Pineapple / Achar 145
Pilaf, Golden Rice 164
pineapple
 Pineapple Curry, with Coconut Milk and Saffron 59
 Spicy Pineapple Pickle / Achar 145
Pineapple Curry with Coconut Milk and Saffron 59
Pineapple Pickle, Spicy / Achar 145
pistachios, crushed
 Falooda 208
Pittu, Arisi-Maa / Steamed Rice Flour and Coconut 188
Pittu, Pal / Steamed Rice Flour and Coconut with Milk 190
Pittu, Spinach / Keerai Pittu 184

plain flour. *See* wheat flour
Plantain Curry, Spicy 65
plantains
  Eggplant, Plantain, and Potato Curry / Kaliya Kari 40
  Plantain Sambol 131
  Spicy Plantain Curry 65
Plantain Sambol 131
plantains, green
  Mild Green Plantain Curry 55
Planter's Tea 207
plum tomatoes. *See* tomatoes, plum
Pol Sambol, or Thengai-Poo / Coconut Sambol 126
pomegranate
  Pumpkin Curry 61
Pongal, Jaggery / Sakkarai Pongal 167
Poritha Ulli Kari / Fried Garlic Curry 42
Poriyal, Asparagus 69
Poriyal, Brussels Sprouts 71
Poriyal, Cauliflower 73
Poriyal, Dried Hibiscus 74
Poriyal, Eggplant, Potato, and Pea Pod 75
Poriyal, Jaffna Whole Eggplant Fry / Yaalpana Kaththarikaii 77
Poriyal, Mixed Vegetable 79
Porridge, Herbal / Kola Kenda 158
Porridge or Pudding, Purple Yam / Irasavalli Kizhangu Kanji 222
potatoes
  Bonda 104
  Coconut Milk Gravy / Sothi 152
  Deviled Potatoes / Urulai Kizhangu 67
  Eggplant, Plantain, and Potato Curry / Kaliya Kari 40
  Eggplant, Potato, and Pea Pod Poriyal 75
  Green Chili Curry / Kari-Milaggai Kari 44
  Masala Potato Filling 182
  Stringhopper Biryani / Idiyappam Biryani 197
  Tempered Potatoes 83
  Vegetable Cutlets 111
Potatoes, Deviled / Urulai Kizhangu 67
Potatoes, Tempered 83
prosecco
  Mango-Passionfruit Punch or Mimosa 211
  Pudding or Porridge, Purple Yam / Irasavalli Kizhangu Kanji 222
pumpkin
  Pumpkin Curry 61
  Vegetable and Lentil Stew / Sambar 96
pumpkin, crystallized
  Love Cake 220
Pumpkin Curry 61
pumpkin curry, prepared
  Curried Pumpkin Soup 156
pumpkin seeds
  Pumpkin Curry 61
  Pumpkin Seeds, Roasted, Sri Lankan-Style 157
pumpkin seeds, white
  Roasted Pumpkin Seeds, Sri Lankan-Style 156
Pumpkin Soup, Curried 156
Punch, Mango-Passionfruit, or Mimosa 211
Purple Yam Pudding or Porridge / Irasavalli Kizhangu Kanji 222

Q

Quick-Pickled Cucumber-Carrot Relish 143

R

raisins
  Jaggery Pongal / Sakkarai Pongal 167
Raita, Cucumber-Tomato 146
Rampé. *See* pandan leaf
red chilies, dried
  Bonda 104
  Chili Onion Sambol / Lunu Miris Sambol 125
  Green Bean Varai 88
  Green Tomato and Lentil Curry 50
  Lentil Patties / Kadalai Vadai 107
  Mango-Ginger Chutney 122
  Okra Curry / Vendikkai Kari 57
  Rose Sambol 133
  Spices and Ingredients 12
  Stir-fried Chickpea Snack / Kadalai Sundal 109

Stir-Fried Semolina / Uppuma 192
Tamarind Rice with Black Lentils 199
Tempered Lentils / Paruppu 81
Tempered Potatoes 83
Vegetable and Lentil Stew / Sambar 96
red chili flakes
   Quick-Pickled Cucumber-Carrot Relish 143
red chilis, fresh
   Pumpkin Curry 61
red lentils, split
   Lentil Patties / Kadalai Vadai 107
Red Rice Congee 176
rhubarb stalks
   Cranberry-Rhubarb Chutney 117
rice, basmati
   Biryani 162
   Golden Rice Pilaf 164
   Savory Rice Pancakes / Thosai 181
rice, cooked
   Herbal Porridge / Kola Kenda 158
   Tamarind Rice with Black Lentils 199
rice flour
   Bonda 104
   Kokis 218
   Lentil Patties / Kadalai Vadai 107
rice flour, red
   Stringhoppers / Idiyappam 194
   Sweet Coconut Steamed Appams / Halapa 228
rice flour, white
   Hoppers / Appam 165
   Stringhoppers / Idiyappam 194
rice flour, white or red
   Steamed Rice Flour and Coconut / Arisi-Maa Pittu 188
   Steamed Rice Flour and Coconut with Milk / Pal Pittu 190
rice, parboiled
   Savory Rice Pancakes / Thosai 181
   Steamed Rice Cakes / Idli 186
Rice Pilaf, Golden 164
rice powder, toasted
   Coconut Milk Gravy / Sothi 152
rice, red
   Red Rice Congee 176
rice, short grain white or red
   Milk Rice / Kiri Bath 172
rice vinegar. *See* vinegar, rice
rice, white or red
   Jaggery Pongal / Sakkarai Pongal 167
   Rich Cake (Wedding / Christmas Cake) 224
   Ripe Jackfruit Curry / Palapazham Kari 63
   Roasted Brussels Sprouts with Jaggery, Balsamic, & Cayenne 94
   Roasted Pumpkin Seeds, Sri Lankan-Style 157
   Rosappu Pachadi / Rose (or Hibiscus) Salad 115
rose essence
   Falooda 208
   Golden Rice Pilaf 164
   Mango Lassi 210
   Purple Yam Pudding or Porridge / Irasavalli Kizhangu Kanji 222
   Spices and Ingredients 16
rose extract
   Rich Cake (Wedding / Christmas Cake) 224
   Rose (or Hibiscus) Salad / Rosappu Pachadi 115
roses
   Rose (or Hibiscus) Salad / Rosappu Pachadi 115
   Rose Sambol 133
Rose Sambol 133
rose water
   Spices and Ingredients 16
rose water extract
   Love Cake 220
Roti, Millet, with Coconut and Jaggery / Kurakkan Roti 174
Roti, Plain / Kothambu Roti 178
rotis
   Chopped Roti Stir-Fry / Kottu Roti 179
Roti Stir-Fry, Chopped / Kottu Roti 179

S

saffron
   Golden Rice Pilaf 164

Jaggery Pongal / Sakkarai Pongal 167
Pineapple Curry, with Coconut Milk and Saffron 59
Tempered Lentils / Paruppu 81
sago. See tapioca pearls
Sakkarai Pongal / Jaggery Pongal 167
Salad, Cucumber 113
Salad, Pickled Beet 114
Salad, Rose (or Hibiscus) / Rosappu Pachadi 115
Salad, Tropical Fruit, with Ginger-Lime Dressing 232
sambar powder
  Spices and Ingredients 16
  Vegetable and Lentil Stew / Sambar 96
Sambar / Vegetable and Lentil Stew 96
Sambol, Bitter Gourd / Paavakkai Sambol 124
Sambol, Chili Onion / Lunu Miris Sambol 125
Sambol, Coconut / Thengai-Poo, or Pol Sambol 126
Sambol, Eggplant / Kaththarikkai Sambol 128
Sambol, Ginger / Injii Sambol 129
Sambol, Kale 130
Sambol, Plantain 131
Sambol, Rose 133
Sambol, Sweet Onion / Seeni Sambol 134
Savory Rice Pancakes / Thosai 181
Seasoned Onions, Master Recipe 20
Seeni Sambol / Sweet Onion Sambol 134
seitan
  Marinated Ginger-Garlic Seitan 91
Sembaruthipoo Kari / Hibiscus (Shoeflower) Curry 52
semolina, coarse
  Stir-Fried Semolina / Uppuma 192
semolina, fine
  Rich Cake (Wedding / Christmas Cake) 224
semolina, toasted
  Love Cake 220
Serendib 207
serrano chili. See green chilies

Sesame Balls / Ellu Urundai / Thala Guli 227
sesame seeds
  Marinated Ginger-Garlic Tofu 90
  Sesame Balls / Ellu Urundai / Thala Guli 227
shallots
  Bottle Gourd and Spinach Curry 32
  Eggplant Pickle / Brinjal Moju 136
  Jaffna Whole Eggplant Fry / Yaalpana Kaththarikaii Poriyal 77
  Marinated Ginger-Garlic Tofu 90
  Plantain Sambol 131
  Spicy Pineapple Pickle / Achar 145
  Spinach Pittu / Keerai Pittu 184
  Stir-fried Chickpea Snack / Kadalai Sundal 109
Sothi / Coconut Milk Gravy 152
Soup, Coriander / Kothamalli Rasam 154
Soup, Curried Pumpkin 156
Spiced Tomato Jam / Thakkaali Yaam 149
Spiced Yogurt Drink / Moru Thanni 213
Spicy Pineapple Pickle / Achar 145
Spicy Plantain Curry 65
spinach, baby
  Bottle Gourd and Spinach Curry 32
spinach, fresh or thawed frozen
  Spinach Pittu / Keerai Pittu 184
Spinach Pittu / Keerai Pittu 184
split legumes. See red lentils, split and urad dal, split
squash
  Biryani 162
  Vegetable and Lentil Stew / Sambar 96
Sri Lankan Curry Powder
  Biryani 162
  Bottle Gourd and Spinach Curry 32
  Cashew Curry / Kaju Kari 35
  Chili-Mango Cashews / Kari-Maangai Kaaju 106
  Drumstick Curry / Murungakkai Kari 36
  Eggplant Curry / Kaththarikkai Kari 38
  Eggplant, Plantain, and Potato Curry / Kaliya Kari 40
  Fried Garlic Curry / Poritha Ulli Kari 42

Green Chili Curry / Kari-Milaggai Kari 44
Green Jackfruit Curry / Palakkai Kari 48
Lime-Masala Mushrooms 89
Mango-Ginger Chutney 122
Okra Curry / Vendikkai Kari 57
Ripe Jackfruit Curry / Palapazham Kari 63
Spices and Ingredients 13
Spicy Plantain Curry 65
Sri Lankan Roasted Pumpkin Seeds 156
Sri Lankan Curry Powder, Master Recipe 18
Sri Lankan Seasoned Onions, Master Recipe 20
Steamed Rice Cakes / Idli 186
Steamed Rice Flour and Coconut / Arisi-Maa Pittu 188
Steamed Rice Flour and Coconut with Milk / Pal Pittu 190
Stew, Vegetable and Lentil / Sambar 96
Stir-fried Chickpea Snack / Kadalai Sundal 109
Stir-Fried Semolina / Uppuma 192
stock, vegetable
  Curried Pumpkin Soup 156
Stringhopper Biryani / Idiyappam Biryani 197
Stringhoppers / Idiyappam 194
sugar
  Beet Juice with Coconut Milk and Lime 202
  Beetroot Cocktail 206
  Broccoli Varai 85
  Coconut Rock / Coconut Ice 216
  Cucumber Salad 113
  Falooda 208
  Fresh Sweet Lime Juice / Thesikkai Saaru 212
  Green Mango Curry / Maankai Kari 46
  Hoppers / Appam 165
  Kale Sambol 130
  Kokis 218
  Mango-Ginger Chutney 122
  Pickled Beet Salad 114
  Plantain Sambol 131
  Purple Yam Pudding or Porridge / Irasavalli Kizhangu Kanji 222
  Quick-Pickled Cucumber-Carrot Relish 143
  Spicy Pineapple Pickle / Achar 145
  Steamed Rice Flour and Coconut with Milk / Pal Pittu 190
  Sweet Onion Sambol / Seeni Sambol 134
sugar, confectioners'
  Love Cake 220
  Rich Cake (Wedding / Christmas Cake) 224
sugar, fine
  Love Cake 220
sugar, rock
  After-Dinner Digestive 234
sultanas
  Biryani 162
  Cranberry-Rhubarb Chutney 117
  Falooda 208
  Golden Rice Pilaf 164
  Green Tomato Chutney with Apples 120
  Mango-Ginger Chutney 122
  Stringhopper Biryani / Idiyappam Biryani 197
  Sweet Coconut Steamed Appams / Halapa 228
sweetening. *See* sugar, jaggery
Sweet Onion Sambol / Seeni Sambol 134
Sweet Thosai / Inippu Thosai 230

T

tamarind juice
  Tamarind Rice with Black Lentils 199
tamarind paste
  Coriander Soup / Kothamalli Rasam 154
  Drumstick Curry / Murungakkai Kari 36
  Eggplant, Plantain, and Potato Curry / Kaliya Kari 40
  Fried Garlic Curry / Poritha Ulli Kari 42
  Ripe Jackfruit Curry / Palapazham Kari 63
  Spices and Ingredients 16
  Vegetable and Lentil Stew / Sambar 96
tamarind pulp
  Sweet Onion Sambol / Seeni Sambol 134
  Tamarind Rice with Black Lentils 199

tapioca pearls
   Falooda 208
tea bags, black Ceylon
   Chai 203
tea, hot black Ceylon
   Planter's Tea 207
tempeh
   Marinated Ginger-Garlic Tempeh 92
Tempered Lentils / Paruppu 81
Tempered Potatoes 83
Thakkaali Yaam / Spiced Tomato Jam 149
Thala Guli / Ellu Urundai / Sesame Balls 227
Thengai Chutney / Green Coconut Chutney 119
Thengai-Poo, or Pol Sambol / Coconut Sambol 126
Thesikkai Saaru / Fresh Sweet Lime Juice 212
Thosai, Kundu / Paniyaram 169
Thosai / Savory Rice Pancakes 181
Thosai, Sweet / Inippu Thosai 230
tofu, extra firm, cubed
   Marinated Ginger-Garlic Tofu 90
tomatoes
   Asparagus Poriyal 69
   Ripe Jackfruit Curry / Palapazham Kari 63
   Spiced Tomato Jam / Thakkaali Yaam 149
   Vegetable and Lentil Stew / Sambar 96
tomatoes, cherry
   Bitter Gourd Sambol / Paavakkai Sambol 124
   Jaffna Whole Eggplant Fry / Yaalpana Kaththarikaii Poriyal 77
   Kale Sambol 130
tomatoes, green
   Green Tomato and Lentil Curry 50
   Green Tomato Chutney with Apples 120
tomatoes, plum
   Cucumber-Tomato Raita 146
Tomato Jam , Spiced / Thakkaali Yaam 149
Tropical Fruit Salad with Ginger-Lime Dressing 232
Tropical Fruit with Chili, Salt, and Lime 233
tulsi

Falooda 208
Spices and Ingredients 16
turmeric
   Beet Curry 31
   Bitter Gourd Sambol / Paavakkai Sambol 124
   Bonda 104
   Bottle Gourd and Spinach Curry 32
   Broccoli Varai 85
   Brussels Sprouts Poriyal 71
   Cabbage Varai / Muttaikoss Varai 87
   Carrot Curry 34
   Cauliflower Poriyal 73
   Coconut Milk Gravy / Sothi 152
   Dried Hibiscus Poriyal 74
   Eggplant Curry / Kaththarikkai Kari 38
   Eggplant Pickle / Brinjal Moju 136
   Eggplant, Plantain, and Potato Curry / Kaliya Kari 40
   Eggplant, Potato, and Pea Pod Poriyal 75
   Eggplant Sambol / Kaththarikkai Sambol 128
   Green Bean Varai 88
   Green Tomato and Lentil Curry 50
   Hibiscus (Shoeflower) Curry / Sembaruthipoo Kari 52
   Jaffna Whole Eggplant Fry / Yaalpana Kaththarikaii Poriyal 77
   Kokis 218
   Leeks Fried with Chili 147
   Lime Pickle 138
   Mango Pickle / Maankai Oorukkai 141
   Marinated Ginger-Garlic Seitan 91
   Marinated Ginger-Garlic Tempeh 92
   Marinated Ginger-Garlic Tofu 90
   Masala Potato Filling 182
   Mild Green Plantain Curry 55
   Mixed Vegetable Poriyal 79
   Okra Curry / Vendikkai Kari 57
   Pineapple Curry, with Coconut Milk and Saffron 59
   Plantain Sambol 131
   Pumpkin Curry 61
   Ripe Jackfruit Curry / Palapazham Kari 63
   Spicy Plantain Curry 65

Stringhopper Biryani / Idiyappam Biryani 197
Tamarind Rice with Black Lentils 199
Tempered Potatoes 83
Vegetable and Lentil Stew / Sambar 96

U

Uppuma / Stir-Fried Semolina 192
urad dal, split
  Kundu Thosai / Paniyaram 169
  Masala Potato Filling 182
  Savory Rice Pancakes / Thosai 181
  Spices and Ingredients 17
  Steamed Rice Cakes / Idli 186
  Tamarind Rice with Black Lentils 199
  Vegetable and Lentil Stew / Sambar 96
Urulai Kizhangu / Deviled Potatoes 67

V

vanilla extract
  Love Cake 220
  Rich Cake (Wedding / Christmas Cake) 224
Varai, Broccoli 85
Varai, Cabbage / Muttaikoss Varai 87
Varai, Green Bean 88
vegan butter. *See* butter, vegan
Vegetable and Lentil Stew / Sambar 96
Vegetable Cutlets 111
vegetable oil
  Bottle Gourd and Spinach Curry 32
  Carrot Curry 34
  Cashew Curry / Kaju Kari 35
  Eggplant Curry / Kaththarikkai Kari 38
vegetable oil for frying
  Bitter Gourd Sambol / Paavakkai Sambol 124
  Bonda 104
  Eggplant Pickle / Brinjal Moju 136
  Eggplant Sambol / Kaththarikkai Sambol 128
  Hibiscus (Shoeflower) Curry / Sembaruthipoo Kari 52
  Jaffna Whole Eggplant Fry / Yaalpana Kaththarikaii Poriyal 77

Kokis 218
Lentil Patties / Kadalai Vadai 107
Marinated Ginger-Garlic Seitan 91
Marinated Ginger-Garlic Tempeh 92
Marinated Ginger-Garlic Tofu 90
Millet Roti, with Coconut and Jaggery / Kurakkan Roti 174
Okra Curry / Vendikkai Kari 57
Plain Roti / Kothambu Roti 178
Plantain Sambol 131
Spicy Plantain Curry 65
Vegetable Cutlets 111
vegetables, frozen mixed
  Mixed Vegetable Poriyal 79
  Vegetable Cutlets 111
vegetable stock
  Curried Pumpkin Soup 156
Vendikkai Kari / Okra Curry 57
vinegar
  Biryani 162
  Eggplant Pickle / Brinjal Moju 136
  Green Mango Curry / Maankai Kari 46
  Mango Pickle / Maankai Oorukkai 141
  Pickled Beet Salad 114
  Plantain Sambol 131
  Spices and Ingredients 17
vinegar, apple cider
  Cranberry-Rhubarb Chutney 117
  Green Tomato Chutney with Apples 120
  Spicy Pineapple Pickle / Achar 145
vinegar, balsamic
  Roasted Brussels Sprouts with Jaggery, Balsamic, and Cayenne 94
vinegar, malt
  Mango-Ginger Chutney 122
vinegar, rice
  Cucumber Salad 113
vinegar, white
  Quick-Pickled Cucumber-Carrot Relish 143

W

Wedding / Christmas Cake (Rich Cake) 224
wheat flour

Steamed Rice Flour and Coconut / Arisi-
    Maa Pittu 188
Steamed Rice Flour and Coconut with
    Milk / Pal Pittu 190
wheat flour and rice flour, mixed
   Hoppers / Appam 165
wheat vermicelli
   Falooda 208
winter squash. *See* pumpkin

Y

Yaalpana Kaththarikaii Poriyal / Jaffna
    Whole Eggplant Fry 77
yams, purple
   Purple Yam Pudding or Porridge / Irasavalli
    Kizhangu Kanji 222
yogurt, vegan
   Cucumber-Tomato Raita 146
   Mango Lassi 210
   Rose (or Hibiscus) Salad / Rosappu
    Pachadi 115
   Spiced Yogurt Drink / Moru Thanni 213

Z

zest. *See* lemon zest, lime zest, orange zest

www.ingramcontent.com/pod-product-compliance
Lightning Source LLC
Chambersburg PA
CBHW071955070526
44583CB00015B/1205